MW01252288

A 100-year look at events that shaped the history of Blue Earth and Nicollet counties from 1900 to 1999

Published by *The Free Press Co*.
Mankato, Minnesota

Published by The Free Press Co.
418 South Second Street
Mankato, MN 56001

Printed in the United States of America

Chronicles of a century : a 100-year look at events that shaped the history of Blue Earth and Nicollet counties from 1900 to 1999 / by The Free Press ; [Sherry Crawford, book editor]. Mankato, MN ; The Free Press Co., c1999.

120 p. : ports. ; 28 cm.

These stories and photos were first published in a special four-part edition of The Free Press in March 1999.

Summary: A collective history of the Mankato, MN, region from 1900 to 1999, featuring photographs and stories of the challenges, natural disasters, and changes that have been a part of the lives of the residents of the Minnesota River valley.

ISBN 0-9675929-0-9

1. Blue Earth County (Minn.)--History. 2. Nicollet County (Minn.)--History. 3. Mankato (Minn.)--History. 4. North Mankato (Minn.)--History. 5. Saint Peter (Minn.)--History. I. Crawford, Sherry. II. Free Press Company (Mankato, Minn.) III. Title.

F612.B6 *99-68345*
977.6--dc21 *CIP*

By studying our history, we come to better understand ourselves–where we came from and how we got here. It can help us learn from our mistakes and plot a better course for tomorrow.

Our history shapes our character as a community, our hardships, struggles, joys and accomplishments. In short, it defines us.

The Mankato region felt echoes of nationwide changes and events: transportation changes, farm crisis, the Great Depression, World War II. Retail expansion that boosted downtowns and brought new malls. Technological innovations that altered agricultural production and the economic base.

But there were also unique stories, of artists who thrived here, such as authors Sinclair Lewis and Maud Hart-Lovelace; successful schools, dairies, stone quarries and clever entrepreneurs.

Residents endured natural disaster and hardship, some from the Minnesota River, an integral element in the community. The 1960s and 1990s brought incredible floods. And a pack of tornadoes descended on the towns of Comfrey and St. Peter–and the rural areas in between–in March 1998, leaving devastation and two dead.

These "Chronicles of a Century" offer a collective history of the Mankato region from 1900 to 1999. They are fascinating stories of challenge, survival and change. They reveal the evolution of a river town, the region's development–and how we became who we are today.

– Sherry Crawford
Book Editor

Acknowledgments

This book would not have been possible without the help of the Blue Earth County and Nicollet County Historical Societies. Their archives provided many of the photos used in this volume.

A portion of the proceeds from the sale of this book will go to the Blue Earth and Nicollet Counties Historical Societies.

These stories and photos were first published in a special four-part edition of *The Free Press* in March 1999. *The Free Press* staff members who compiled this edition include:

Writers - Shelley Croes, Mark Fischenich, Tim Krohn, Robb Murray, Brian Ojanpa, Peter Passi, Rebecca Richter, Jody Sailor and Joe Tougas.

Photographers - John Cross and Brett Groehler.

Editors - Greg Abbott, Deb Flemming, David Norris, Joe Spear, Carol Svendsen, Edward Thoma and Kathy Vos.

Contents

Chronicles of a Century

Part 1

1900 - 1925

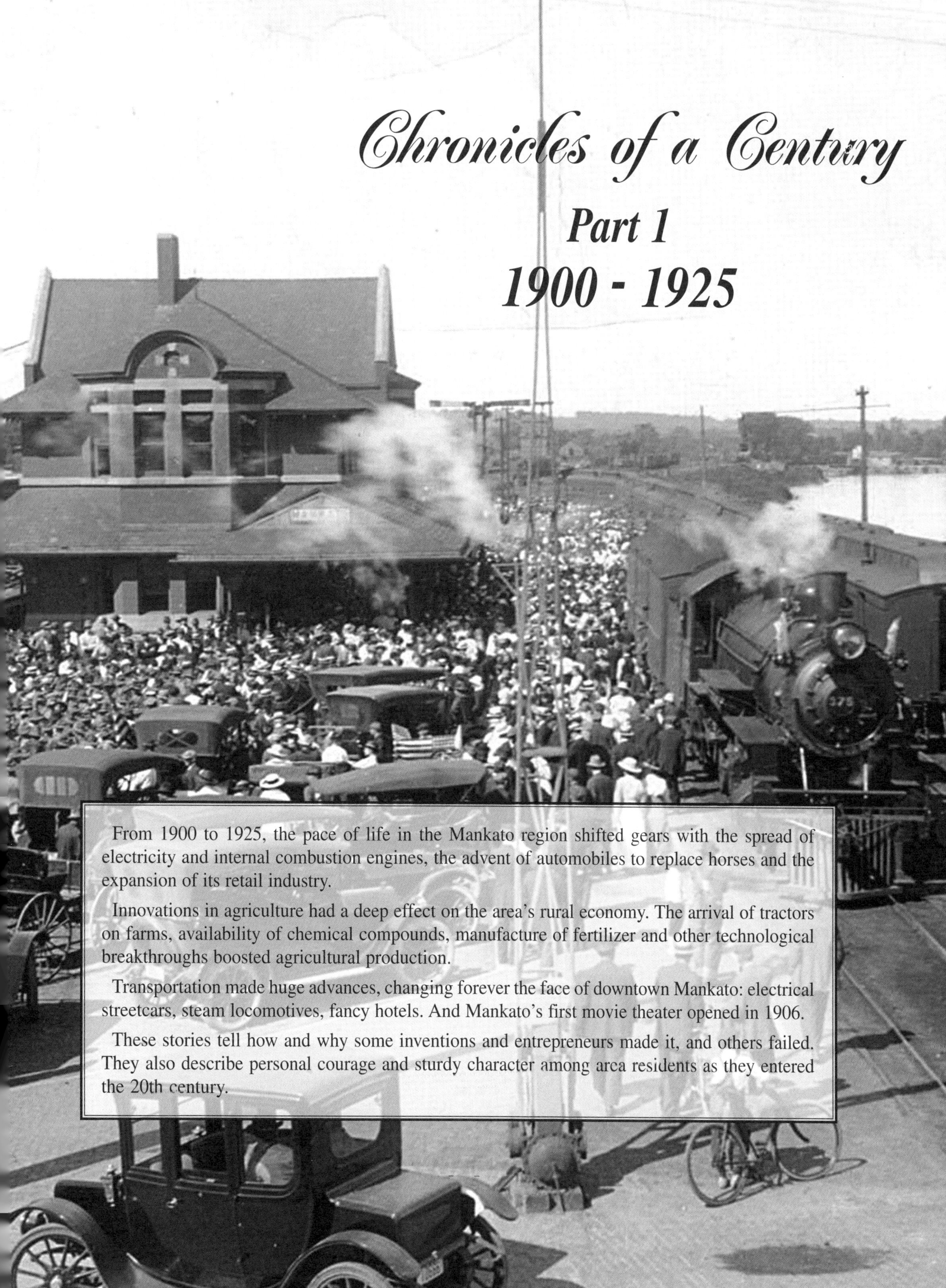

From 1900 to 1925, the pace of life in the Mankato region shifted gears with the spread of electricity and internal combustion engines, the advent of automobiles to replace horses and the expansion of its retail industry.

Innovations in agriculture had a deep effect on the area's rural economy. The arrival of tractors on farms, availability of chemical compounds, manufacture of fertilizer and other technological breakthroughs boosted agricultural production.

Transportation made huge advances, changing forever the face of downtown Mankato: electrical streetcars, steam locomotives, fancy hotels. And Mankato's first movie theater opened in 1906.

These stories tell how and why some inventions and entrepreneurs made it, and others failed. They also describe personal courage and sturdy character among area residents as they entered the 20th century.

Retailing changed with power

Electricity extended business hours; autos stretched market area

Bicycles and horse-drawn carts still dominated the streets of downtown Mankato in 1904. This shot is of Front Street, looking south. Note that Mankato's busiest thoroughfare still had not been paved.

During the first quarter of this century, the spread of electricity and the internal combustion engine began to transform the downtown faces of cities such as Mankato, North Mankato and St. Peter.

Nonstop 24-hour electric service became available in Mankato in 1901, and by 1910 most residents had ready access to power. Electricity extended retailers' business hours and created demand for a host of revolutionary new products.

The internal combustion engine brought new business to cities and changed the way people shopped.

As the century began, horses and carts still outnumbered automobiles on the streets of southern Minnesota.

The downtowns of Mankato, St. Peter and North Mankato reflected the continued importance of four-legged transport. Harness makers, blacksmiths and cart builders did brisk business.

In 1900, Mankato was home to nine liveries.

The Mankato harness shop Gottlieb Schmidt opened in 1859 was still selling mostly tackle at the turn of the century.

Later, as fewer people used horses, the shop diversified its product line, moving into sales of purses and luggage, as well as horse handling goods.

Hotels, such as the three-story Stahl House on Mankato's North Front Street, maintained liveries. After all, travelers needed to arrange accommodations for their horses, as well as themselves.

Mankato boasted lavish lodging places. The Stahl House, for instance, was steam heated, offering 41 sleeping rooms, a parlor, dining room and bathrooms on each floor.

But such accommodations didn't come cheap. Guests during the early 1900s paid from $1 to $1.50 for a night's stay.

Other Mankato hotels of the era included the City Hotel, the Hotel Heinrich with its upscale Palm Room for diners, the Clifton House, the Washington House, the Ben Pay Hotel and the grand Saulpaugh Hotel.

St. Peter also had a healthy lodging industry. Hotels included the Nicollet House, the Commercial, the Northwestern and the Union House.

Hotels were centers of commerce, as well as lodging. Traveling salesmen arrived by railroad and often set up shop for a week at a stretch in local inns. From 1920 through the 1940s, more than 20 passenger trains, carrying shoppers and salesmen, arrived daily in Mankato. The busy railroad ticket office was open around the clock.

Some hotels, such as Mankato's Hotel Heinrich, came to the railroad depot with horse-drawn carriages to pick up guests and their luggage.

Mankato's biggest draw, however, continued to be its downtown shops. The city was home to about 35 tailors, 48 dressmakers and a number of milliners (hatmakers). Stores proliferated along Front Street, which ran parallel to the Minnesota River and the railroad tracks.

Several department stores were operating during the first quarter of 1900. Some of the first and most dominant of the era were homegrown businesses.

George E. Brett opened his Empire Store in 1868 with the help of $3,000 he borrowed from his father-in-law, then mayor of St. Paul. His 22-by-22-foot shop stood on Front Street between Jackson and Cherry streets.

By 1910, the store had outgrown its quarters and relocated to the northeast corner of Front and Jackson. From then on, the store was known as Brett's.

The well-appointed department store provided customers with certain luxuries. It maintained an upstairs lounge, complete with couches and writing tables for those who tired of shopping.

Brett Taylor Jr., great-grandson of George E. Brett, said the sitting room reflected the pace of the times.

"Many people came to Mankato from small towns in horse-drawn wagons. They would spend the day here, and to have a place where they could sit down and rest made sense."

Mankato had other department stores, including Salet's, established by Leon Salet in 1896, and JC Penney, which arrived downtown in 1917.

History Glance
1900s

A force in timber

St. Peter was known for its lumberyards at the turn of the century.

Roscoe Horton established his first of what would be many building supply outlets–Standard Lumber Co.–at the corner of Grace Street and Minnesota Avenue. Horton would later acquire more than 36 lumberyards scattered throughout Minnesota.

Jake and Leonard Lampert opened a building center of their own nearby, at the corner of Grace and Third streets. Their business, too, would mushroom into multiple stores.

On the dry side

In 1900, North Mankato residents voted to disallow any businesses that sold alcohol, and the city remained dry through the first quarter of the century.

Mankato was more of a free-wheeling city. It had 35 saloons before Prohibition was declared in 1920.

In 1900, the Mankato Board of Trade estimated local retail sales totaled about $6.5 million.

There were no credit cards during this era, but many merchants, keeping track of purchases by way of a ledger book, did extend credit to customers.

"If you had customers who were farmers, you knew they wouldn't get paid until they took their crops to market. You just carried them until then," Taylor said.

By the early 1900s, St. Peter had its own full complement of businesses, including grocers, bakers, tailors, harness makers and other flourishing small shops.

Shop owners were often quick to respond to whatever a customer needed. The Klein Furniture Shop of St. Peter, founded in 1856, was a place where you could order a wardrobe, a dining room table or–when the time came–a coffin.

Craftsmen at Klein's gladly offered their services and carpentry skills to grieving families. Eventually the funeral business eclipsed furniture-making altogether.

To survive, retailers had to adapt to customers' changing needs and tastes. Shops were often quite eclectic as a result. The shop established by Julius Ritt, a German immigrant who settled in St. Peter, is a good illustration.

Shortly before the turn of the century, Ritt opened a gun repair shop on a shoestring budget with a few secondhand tools. Soon, he began to sell new guns and ammunition. Next, he added bicycles to his inventory.

In 1909, Ritt's began to carry Edison phonographs and recordings. The business also evolved into an outlet for lighting appliances, musical instruments and then motorcycles.

A young George Enfield leaned on a display case inside his family's shop at 629 N. Front Street, Mankato. Dry goods stores like this one, operated by Ed and Julia Enfield, were fixtures in downtown Mankato and St. Peter during the first quarter of the century.

In 1868, George E. Brett opened his Empire Store on Front Street between Jackson and Cherry streets. But by 1910, the business had outgrown the building, and Brett's relocated to the northeast corner of Front and Jackson.

Electric street cars came to Mankato streets in '08

Mode of transit died out in city by 1930 as autos gained popularity

The 1900s saw the heyday of streetcars in Mankato, as they had evolved at that point from being horse-driven to being electronically driven. A lack of riders caused street cars to vanish by the 1930s.

The first streetcars in Mankato were of the horse-drawn variety.

Their era began in 1886 on a June day, with nearly 1,000 people on the first run of the Mankato Street Railway streetcar, headed down Front Street. The venture began with an initial investment of $50,000 by two prominent businessmen, William M. Farr and John C. Noe. Four horse-drawn cars rode from 6:30 a.m. to 10 p.m. daily.

But people seemed reluctant to ride the horse-drawn cars. Historian Thomas Hughes wrote in his book "History of Blue Earth County" that "Mankato at that time proved too small a town for a street railway, and the patronage failed to pay the operating expense. The company finally, in 1895, surrendered their franchise, pulled up their tracks and abandoned the project."

Then in 1906, courtesy of the Mankato Electric Traction Co., streetcars came back, this time driven by electricity. On a cold day in May 1908, Mankato was abuzz with people ready to pay nickels to ride the streetcar. The first riders were Glen and Mert Dobbins of 913 S. Front St.

Routes ran from Tourtellotte to Sibley parks, up to Mankato Normal School and over to west Mankato. Streetcars, however, fell victim to the growing popularity of automobiles. By 1930, they disappeared.

History Glance
1900s

Smithy forges his way
Power drills, grinders, a lathe and forges were among the equipment found at Frank Wild's progressive blacksmith and wagon making business in North Mankato.

"Mr. Wild is an expert smithy, having followed the trade for many years, and his shop is headquarters for farmers, who find the best of everything needed in their work for sale here at very reasonable prices," the Mankato Daily Free Press wrote earlier in the century.

Wild also carried sample farm machinery of the most popular makes: Parlin & Orndorf implements, wagons and buggies; Page fencing; Jackson fencing; Iowa and automatic cream separators; standard hay tools; Louden's barn equipment; and Stillwater machine–made twine.

A sweet place
One business that was a favorite with children of all ages was the Mankato Candy Kitchen, established in 1903 by Chris Zotalis. The store made and sold its own rock salt ice cream and confections.

Saturday was shopping day

St. Peter bustled with farmers bartering produce for the goods they sought

This is the interior of the Baberich store, which was located on the west side of St. Peter's Minnesota Avenue between Grace and Nassau streets.

Each Saturday, Minnesota Avenue would fill with activity as families poured into St. Peter to purchase their weekly provisions.

"Saturday was the big shopping day," said Bob Wettergren, lifelong resident of St. Peter and local history buff.

Many of the customers from neighboring farms bought what they needed without a dime. Wettergren said many grocers bartered with farmers, accepting produce in exchange for other goods.

Probably the hottest retail space in St. Peter around the turn of the century was in a brick building Dr. A.W. Daniels constructed in 1899, Wettergren said.

It housed three street-level storefronts and Daniels rented the upper level to the Masons.

Daniels was a widely renowned doctor, Wettergren said.

"In his day, he was more famous than the Mayos."

The Mayo brothers, who would later founded the Mayo Clinic, owned land north of town, near Le Sueur.

Besides being one of the newer structures in town, the Daniels' building had location working in its favor.

"The 300 block has always been the premier block in town," Wettergren said.

The block was home to the Baberich Dry Goods Store, the Philip Dick clothing store and the Adolphson shoe store.

In the 1920s, Pete Schuveiller bought out the Baberiches and expanded the inventory.

"My grandmother bought everything from Pete Schuveiller," Wettergren recalled. "He would put down a stool for her and she'd spend all afternoon in his store."

Schuveiller struck up friendships with regular customers and didn't always concern himself strictly with business. Schuveiller sometimes invited male customers into the back of the store, Wettergren said.

"Pete liked to drink, and he kept a jug back there."

Although the Constitution's 18th amendment, passed in 1919, outlawed alcohol consumption, St. Peter was hardly a dry town during the years of Prohibition.

"Nobody ever went thirsty around here," Wettergren said.

St. Peter's brewery, Engesser, had been reduced to producing nonalcoholic near-beer, but its product often was augmented locally with grain alcohol. St. Peter had been home to 17 saloons, and while those establishments no longer could openly serve alcohol, Wettergren said patrons could usually arrange to have their beverages spiked.

Mankato residents also found ways to circumvent Prohibition.

Chuck Pennington recalls ducking into the Rex Pool Hall as a boy to check a board that tracked baseball games, inning by inning.

Pool and baseball scores weren't the only things that drew people to the pool hall, however.

"The bootleggers would hang out there," Pennington said.

He recalls a couple of local characters by the names of Koozer and Paige whose jackets were always lined with half-pint bottles of grain alcohol that sold for $2 a pop. There was no shortage of customers even at such a steep price.

"It seems like they were about the only ones that had any money in those days," Pennington said.

But the life of a bootlegger had its dangers. Pennington said that one day Koozer disappeared, and his body was found later stuffed inside a culvert.

Beverages of a more innocent sort were of greater interest to Pennington and his peers, the sorts of drinks sold at popular hangouts such as the American Beauty soda fountain and the Mankato Candy Kitchen. Bottled soda pop had not yet appeared on the scene.

Chris Zotalis and his crew at the Candy Kitchen made their own chocolates and ice cream on the premises. Pennington said the shop offered a stunning variety of ice cream flavors: vanilla, chocolate and strawberry.

Three movie theaters also drew people into downtown Mankato: the State, Town and Grand.

If you wanted popcorn for a show, Pennington recalled, you bought it from a popcorn wagon on the street for a nickel per bag.

History Glance
1900s

A gift from Carnegie

Mankato received a substantial cultural opportunity in 1901, when philanthropist Andrew Carnegie offered the city $40,000 to build a public library, provided a site was furnished and the city provide $4,000 a year and upkeep. The city agreed to the terms.

Carnegie, an immigrant to the United States, gave millions to libraries nationwide and in the United Kingdom. The building in Mankato stands today as the Carengie Art Center, 120 S. Broad St.

Two horse power

Prominent Mankato businessman J. M. Halfhill, who owned a local mercantile, used an odd horse-and-buggy contraption to get around in the early 1900s.

The vehicle, called a skeleton wagon, was just that: a crude version of a traditional horse-drawn four-wheeled wagon. Halfhill used two Arabian horses to pull his rig.

Transportation moves ahead

First quarter of the century was marked by shift to automobiles

Steam locomotives were one of the dominant forms of transportation in the early 1900s. The Dan Patch line, shown here in a photo taken in the 1910s, was one of the area's major people and freight carriers.

It was a time when the automobile was a mere curiosity. And horses were getting spelled by electric street cars. A new iron bridge linked Mankato and North Mankato. And the first pavement was spread on local roads.

The beginning of the 20th century was an exciting time for American transportation, and local citizens were right on pace with the rest of the country.

By 1900, transportation by boat had all but died with the final Minnesota River voyage of the steamship Henrietta, and now people looked mostly to land machines to get around.

Automobiles, invented the late 1800s, were becoming more common as the new century continued. One local man even got into the act, creating a series of automobiles called Kato Cars in his downtown garage.

By 1912 there were nine automobile dealers and repair shops in Mankato, including the precursor company to today's Clements Auto. Service stations also popped up, such as Mankato Oil in 1920.

The first taxi cabs hit the streets in the 1910s. The service was refined by 1924 when six cabs began offering nonstop trips daily between Mankato and Minneapolis. The fare: $2.50.

Buses came to St. Peter in the 1920s, taking people all over the region and, with transfers, all the way to both coasts.

Streetcars also had a brief period of prosperity. In the late 1800s they were pulled by horses. But with the new century came advances in electronic technology and the ability to run electric streetcars around Mankato.

In 1908, the Mankato Electric Traction Co. ran tracks from all over town that included stops at Tourtellotte Park, Sibley Park, west Mankato and Mankato Teachers College.

The life of the streetcar, however, was shortened by the surging popularity of automobiles and small number of local residents to use public transportation.

Trains also had a major presence in the early part of the century. Companies such as the Dan Patch line announced establishment of regular commuter trips between Mankato and

Minneapolis, with stops at Waterville, Faribault and Northfield. Dan Patch, incidentally, went out of business soon after starting passenger runs. Lines such as Chicago Great Western and Milwaukee Road prospered for decades.

St. Peter's train system had rail lines linking it with Mankato and the rest of the state. Residents there often took excursions to Mankato or St. Paul. Those who did were mentioned on the society pages of area newspapers.

Trains were not without their danger. In 1925, M. C. Goodahl, an engineer, was run over by a train trying to couple two cars. He slipped on the track and his arm was severed, shoulder severely cut and legs crushed. He died a few days later in St. Paul.

Airplanes, mostly biplanes, remained a curiosity. A few were spotted in area skies, but planes wouldn't become a dominant presence until World War II.

The most primitive form of transportation, walking, also got some updating. In 1897, the Iron Bridge between Mankato and North Mankato was built, replacing an old ferry bridge that floated from shore to shore on rope rails.

Then in 1917, increasing vehicle traffic prompted another new bridge. The Main Street bridge, a concrete and iron structure that would last 67 years, established three traffic lanes between the towns and provided an economic boon to a fledgling North Mankato. At the time of completion, it was the largest bridge in Minnesota.

History Glance
1900s

Business smoking

The Mankato Cigar Co. was a booming enterprise in 1901, according to The Free Press. Eighteen employees couldn't keep up with demand, including an order for 100,000 placed by the "largest grocery house in the world." Three more workers were reportedly on the way.

"The genial proprietors, Messrs. Achard and Totten, are more than gratified at the enormity of business so far," the newspaper reported, "and hope to continue to merit a large patronage by the manufacturing of good smokers."

No movies on Sunday

Sunday movies were banned for a while in 1909. The city passed a law forbidding shows on the Sabbath.

On March 10, Judge W.L. Comstock fined D.W. Chamberlain $10 for violating the law. The Legislature eventually approved a bill permitting Sunday movies.

Concrete, stone helped build town

Flour was the leading product of Mankato - and rock and concrete second

Local industry employed people and generated wealth by digging into the earth along the Minnesota River Valley and selling stone, gravel, sand, brick and cement. Quarrying and cutting limestone was Mankato's second most important industry just after the turn of the century, surpassed only by the production of flour.

It was 1902 and the Mankato Sidewalk Co. was proud enough of its new product line to run an ad in *The Free Press.*

"Wonderful progress has been made during the 50 years of Mankato's existence," the ad proclaimed, "but that made in the construction of sidewalks is the equal of any line of business. It is no longer necessary to walk in a path or in the middle of the road ... The cement walks being laid in our city by the Mankato Sidewalk Co. will stand as monuments of our progress when Mankato celebrates her centennial anniversary 50 years hence."

On the city's 50th birthday in 1902, getting grandiose about cement probably wasn't bad advertising. This newfangled technology was challenging the town's foundation.

Flour may have been the leading product manufactured in Mankato, but stone and related products were a bedrock element of the local economy.

Quarrying of limestone began in 1853, the year after the bend of the Minnesota River was first settled. Sawmills, flour mills, brick plants and furniture makers followed.

Even by the turn of the century, the town's economy was still based largely on pulling things from the earth, processing them in some minimal way and selling them.

The Mankato Board of Trade reported in 1902 the city's 1900 sales figures for local manufacturers.

Flour was king, with local mills producing 257,000 barrels worth $844,000. More than 10,000 carloads of stone valued at $408,000 came in second, followed by $150,000 worth of hosiery produced by the knitting mills and $131,000 for 876,000 pounds of candy. Feed, beer and bakery goods also topped $100,000 in sales.

Production of cement, barrels, clothing, forged metal products, lime and brick also made the list, each topping $30,000 in sales.

By the turn of the century, Mankato products could be easily exported from the region with good railroad service already well-established. So it wasn't necessarily the case that all 16,000 barrels of beer produced by local brewers were consumed locally.

The William Bierbauer brewery at the head of Rock Street was the first and most successful beer producer. Although eight more followed its establishment in 1857, the Bierbauer brewery was the only one remaining when Prohibition took effect in 1920.

The beverage industry also produced the City Bottling Works and Mankato Mineral Spring Water, which used Le Ray Township springs to produce "positively the best mineral water in the Northwest."

It would have been an understandably thirsty town in those years with days at the quarries and lime kilns described by one worker as "backbreaking and filled with stone dust." As railroads expanded west into the prairie and beyond in the years before the turn of the century, stone was in enormous demand for use in the foundations of trestles.

But the railroads discovered the wonders of concrete in the early years of the 20th century, and by 1915 most of the city's 16 quarries, which employed up to 800 stone cutters and masons at one point, had shut down. After World War I, demand for dimension stone and the increasing use of Mankato stone for decorative purposes on buildings resurrected the industry.

The first 25 years of this century also saw the establishment of local utilities with Mankato Citizens Telephone having outgrown its original location in 1901, just three years after its founding. That was also the first year that 24-hour electric service was available in Mankato, although it wasn't distributed citywide until around 1910.

In 1911, the Rapidan Dam was completed, providing hydroelectric power to Mankato, which soon became part of the Northern State's Power Co. electric grid.

While technology brought new businesses to town, it killed off many and forced others to adapt. The Kuehne Wagon Co. at Second and Mulberry streets became a repair shop after World War I as the growing popularity of automobiles surpassed what was once the area's top producer of horse-drawn vehicles.

History Glance
1900s

Beer and hangings

The Standard Brewing Company of Mankato lasted less than a decade, closing in 1908, but managed to connect beer drinking and memories of the execution of the 38 Dakota Indians.

"The Standard Brewery gave several quality souvenirs to its customers during its brief span of business," the Mankato Review reported. "One of these was a round metal serving tray with a picture in the inner circle depicting the Execution of the Sioux. Another was a rectangular tray, which was a wooden frame with handles and had a glass top surface. A picture showing the Execution of the Sioux was under the glass. Originally, the story of the Sioux Uprising was glued to the wooden bottom of the tray to give a more complete story of the Sioux Uprising and the subsequent execution of the thirty-eight Sioux in Mankato."

North Kato had early industrial roots

Nelsen Contruction Co. had hand in building MSU, Gustavus and Bethany

The A.L. Wheeler and O.E. Bennett brick factory was the first industry to locate in North Mankato in 1886. Workers pose at the brickyard around 1895.

Mankato may have had the mortar materials, but North Mankato was home to a number of brickyards that helped formed the city's landscape during the start of the century.

In fact, the first industry to locate in North Mankato in 1886 was a brick factory, owned by A.L. Wheeler and O.E. Bennett, at present-day Wheeler Park.

Others soon followed, taking advantage of the city's clay resources, including the W.E. Stewart (Mankato Brick and Tile), Shingles and the North Mankato Brick and Tile companies.

Building up the new city was a priority for North Mankato's founding fathers. That was reflected in the makeup of the North Mankato City Council: only three residents who weren't contractors served as council presidents from 1898 to 1923.

Among the council's contractor presidents were Q.M. Hagwell, a lumber contractor who built the 1904 addition to the North Mankato School; J.B. Nelsen, a building contractor who also owned a quarry along the bluff; and Otto Neitge, another successful building contractor.

J. B. Nelsen Construction Co. was established in 1894 by Nelsen, who was considered a progressive but conservative businessman. His company built many public and private buildings in North and South Dakota, Iowa and Minnesota.

"Nearly all of the most prominent buildings in Mankato were constructed by the Nelsen Construction Co.," according to a report of the day. "The list of construction work in the 20 years of business runs over $3 million."

Nelsen's firm constructed the Carnegie Library in Mankato, Immanuel Hospital, the First National Bank, some of Mankato State University's lower campus, Bethany College and Good Counsel Academy in Mankato.

The company also built Gustavus Adolphus College and the Church of St. Peter in St. Peter in 1912. The church took a year to build and cost $40,000.

Nelsen served as the village president from 1900 to 1901, 1903, 1907, 1912 to 1913 and 1915-16.

Another early official, J.A. Tidland, developed a grading and excavating business after he received patents for several motorized pieces of equipment, including a rotary grader and ditcher.

His company dug a 10-mile ditch in the summer of 1901, for which he reportedly received $1,000 a mile.

In 1907, the Stewart brickyard employed 28 men. It cost $67 a day to run the brickyard, according to a ledger.

St. Peter had its own building resources, including the Standard Lumber Co., Lampert Lumber Co., the St. Peter Sidewalk Co. and the St. Peter Cement Construction Co.

At the time, Standard Lumber was one of the largest chain lumber yards in the state, started in 1894 by a group of enterprising young men who had worked in lumbering.

Lampert Lumber Co., later known as the Lampert Building Center, was founded by Jake and Leonard Lampert around 1895. A.M. Jensen bought an interest in the firm in 1916, causing its name change to Jensen and Lampert for a short time.

The St. Peter Stone Sidewalk Co., owned by the Carlson Brothers, laid miles of sidewalk in St. Peter, along with foundations for hundreds of homes and buildings in the city.

The company also laid pipes "for the drainage boom here 15 years ago and earlier," according to a 1930 edition of the *St. Peter Herald*.

1900s

45 own cars in county

As of July 17, 1907, a survey of property by the Blue Earth County assessor showed that just 45 people in the county owned automobiles. But auto dealers were proliferating in the region, and car sales would accelerate quickly.

In the mid-1910s, H.B. Seitzer, who had been helping manufacture Little Giant tractors in Mankato, opened a car dealership in St. Peter. His biggest seller was the Ford Model T. It came in one color. You guessed it–black.

By 1917, Seitzer decided to sell new Fords exclusively.

In 1916, the Mankato Motor Sales Co. announced that it would begin selling King and Dort cars in Mankato. An article in The Free Press said, "The Dort is a light car and sells at $650 F.O.B. [free on board] Mankato, and is a five-passenger car fully equipped." The pricing for an eight-cylinder King started at $1,150.

A rural teacher faces hardships

Ornery cattle were only part of the hardships teachers faced in area

Pleasant Grove was an early elementary school in Mankato.

In the early 1920s, young teacher Effie Holteen encountered an angry bull on her two-mile walk to school in rural Nicollet County.

As the bull prepared to charge, the story has it, she looked around the open field for a place to hide and found refuge behind a wooden gate until the bull grew bored and wandered off.

Teaching was not an easy life.

Young women typically paid about a quarter of their earnings to be boarded in a stranger's home near their school. The rural school buildings were particularly sparse and teachers had to cope with bad weather, limited transportation and few supplies.

Teachers and students in rural schools had to kindle fires and haul fresh water from a nearby farm. If students didn't keep their lunch pails near the front of the room, close to the fire, their lunches would freeze in the winter.

The area's history of schools reads like a construction manual: they were built and replaced, built and replaced. Makeshift schools were common: at the turn of the century, North Mankato's 1,000 residents sent their children to classrooms above a grocery store, which later became a liquor store.

Even early in the century, however, the accommodations were a notch above the first schools. Mankato's first public school was a one-room log cabin built in 1855 for 37 students.

Rapid population growth made schools too small, and new ones were built quickly. By 1902, Mankato's enrollment hit 1,750 students. The district already had six buildings.

Rural schools were built at a rapid rate. State law allowed a school district to be formed in a township if there were at least five families living there, and the district could split if there were more than 10 families. Rural schools, therefore, popped up everywhere.

Residents typically forgot their rural district's official number, and the country schools often took on the name of the nearest farmer. Holteen, the teacher who hid from the bull, taught in what was called the Robert Meyer School District.

Many students dropped out after the eighth grade, and teaching standards weren't high early in the century. Young women often taught at one-room schools until they married. Men, too, took teaching jobs–at substantially higher pay. Contracts were on a year-to-year basis, so teachers didn't know until spring whether they would be welcomed back the next year.

Churches also opened their own schools. They were started and replaced with about the same frequency as the earlier public schools.

By the turn of the century, many of the area's well-known educational institutions were already established. Loyola High School was founded in 1876; and Mankato Normal School, now Minnesota State University, had established itself in 1867 as a teacher training site.

Gustavus Adolphus College was still a relatively new but important addition to St. Peter, having opted to move there in 1876. The college also considered locating in Minneapolis, but St. Peter residents offered $10,000 to help build Old Main. The building stands to this day, even after the March 29, 1998, tornadoes.

Bethany Lutheran College began during this time as a young woman's seminary in 1911. The seminary was purchased in 1927 by a group of pastors and presented to the Norwegian Synod. The school became a coeducational high school and junior college.

Eagle Lake students in a turn-of-the-century photo in their school.

History Glance
1900s

Clothing in St. Peter

St. Peter was home to two clothing manufacturers: Johnson Manufacturing Co. and Home Dress Manufacturing Co.

The Johnson company was established on the site of the old City Hall building in St. Peter in 1896. The building was intended to be used for the state Capitol when community leaders were vying to relocate the state offices here.

Overalls were a specialty of the company, which also produced shirts and pants.

The Home company, on Park Row near the Nicollet Hotel, manufactured house dresses, aprons, middle blouses and other items starting in 1909.

Fire hit businesses

Fires took a toll on Mankato's retail and service community during the first quarter of this century. The City Hotel on Second and Plum streets burned down April 19, 1913. The building was destroyed and the financial loss estimated at $15,000.

Name changes for school? It's Normal

Mankato Normal School was renamed Mankato Teachers College in 1921

By the 1920s parents and school officials were injecting a little more fun into school. Nicollet County kids played on their school's new swing.

Minnesota State University underwent its first name change in 1921, when it gained greater stature by becoming a state teachers college.

Momentum for the change had been building. Mankato Normal School, its original name, was established in 1868. But the school's staff had bigger goals in mind.

In the early 1900s, normal schools typically trained elementary teachers, while high school teachers were trained at universities and private schools. It's no surprise that the conversion to a college was a political battle because these new colleges would drain resources and students from other teacher training programs.

There weren't many Normal graduates who went on to participate in legislative committees, since most elementary teachers were women. Unlike male high school teachers, the female teachers' careers typically ended with marriage; and they didn't become active in political debates.

As the debate waged, Mankato Normal began taking steps. In 1916, it began requiring a high school diploma for admission (many in that time dropped out of school after eighth grade) and added programs that took an extra year of training, such as a junior high component.

The Legislature finally allowed the state's Normals to become teacher colleges in 1921, after rejecting the idea 10 years earlier. But the four-year program took planning. A fire in the school's main building in 1922 aggravated the problem. A new building wasn't constructed until 1924 (the building is now Old Main, a retirement complex for senior citizens).

In 1930, the new Mankato Teachers' College offered its first full four-year degree curriculum.

Teacher pay varied widely

Teachers' salaries in the early part of the century depended on where you taught and whether you wore a skirt.

In Nicollet County in 1915, the average salary for a man teaching in a rural school was $60 a month. A woman earned $48.25 a month. Rural schools typically had an eight-month calendar because children needed to help on the farm.

Wages in town schools were better, but the school calendar was nine months. Men earned an average salary of $85 a month while women earned an average of $52 a month.

Illness a regular problem in early years of century

Outbreaks of smallpox, diphtheria, typhoid fever plagued area for years

Infectious disease could bring school lessons to a halt for days, even weeks, in the days before vaccines and antibiotics were developed.

Around the turn of the century, the opening of North Mankato's new school was cut short by illness. The school was closed shortly after it opened because of cases of black diphtheria.

In 1907 and 1908, there were several epidemics of smallpox and typhoid fever in Blue Earth and Nicollet counties. Families from across the region came to Mankato to receive the smallpox vaccine.

World War I brought a deadly flu epidemic, then called the Spanish influenza. Unlike most flu strains, this bug was as likely to kill its young, healthy victims as the weak. In North Mankato, officials closed the school and library and prohibited public gatherings in October 1917. Mankato and other towns also halted public activities.

By 1918, officials were calling it the worst epidemic in the area's history–worse than typhoid and smallpox. Minnesota and other parts of the country faced the same problem with the flu. Area schools were again closed for more than a week, and a corps of 17 nurses set up a station at Bethany and treated influenza patients.

As vaccines and treatments for these infectious diseases became common, outbreaks were infrequent. Polio, however, was still a dreaded disease for many years.

Tractors get traction on local farms

The average size of a Blue Earth County farm in 1922 was just 160 acres

The Nick Scherer and Nathan Day threshing crew are pictured here at the Quiggle farm north of Amboy at the turn of the century.

The first 25 years of the century brought amazing advances in agriculture. Farming was already the dominant economic and social force in southern Minnesota, and major technological breakthroughs were transforming the industry.

The rich, black soil of Blue Earth and Nicollet counties had drawn thousands of farmers who were each year putting more prairie under the plow. By 1922 there were already 335,347 acres under cultivation in Blue Earth County alone.

But the farms were small by today's standards (averaging about 160 acres, compared to a statewide average of 350 acres today), the work arduous and the production limited.

In the early 1900s it took nine farmers to produce enough food to feed themselves and one city family. (Today, a single farmer feeds more than 60 other people.)

But science and engineering helped ease the workload and boost production.

One of the first tractors–the Hart-Parr No. 1–went into production in 1901 and the debate was soon raging over whether tractors could replace horses. There was major skepticism about tractors, and with good reason: they were huge, inefficient and costly machines.

A 1922 letter to the editor of a local newspaper noted that it cost about $4 a day to operate a six-horse team, while a tractor cost twice as much. (The farmer conceded, however, that the tractor could plow about nine acres a day, three times what the horse team could.)

But as tractors improved, they were quickly added to local farms. A 1920 Minnesota Farm Census listed 200 tractors in Nicollet County, more than any other county statewide.

Meanwhile, scientists were working on improving grain production.

Local farmers grew mostly wheat, oats, hay and some corn in the first quarter of the century.

In 1910, chemical compounds such as calcium arsenate, copper, and sulfur were first used to control the horrible problem of insect infestation in grain.

Fertilizer manufacturing was also beginning in earnest in the early 1900s, and scientists were discovering ways to grow hybrid grain seeds that produced better crops. By the 1920s, there were seed hybridization programs in Minnesota and other states.

The initial mechanical and scientific discoveries of the first 25 years of the century set the stage for rapid improvements that were to come on the farm, especially during World War II, when scientific research accelerated to improve food production.

Gasoline engines ease burden on farm women

Engines power washers, wringers, vacuum cleaners, even sewing machines

In the early 1900s, the advent of the gasoline engine began revolutionizing agriculture, bringing gas-powered tractors and other machinery to rural areas.

But the engine also changed the lives of farm wives.

"Never has there been a machine on the farm which has lightened woman's work as much as the gasoline engine," said a 1915 Farm Power magazine article on the benefits of gasoline engines for home use.

"Instead of a life of drudgery for the farmer's wife and daughter, they can now have free moments for recreation and the better things of life."

One of the biggest benefits was hooking an engine to the washing machine, cutting laundry time in half. The wringer could also be operated by engine, eliminating the grueling work of hand operating the wringer.

The use of gasoline-powered vacuum cleaners was described as having the amazing ability to "draw the dirt by suction from the corners of the room, instead of just stirring it up to settle back again on floors."

The vacuums were hooked to gasoline engines, often mounted on small wagons so they could be pulled around the house.

The story also listed other uses for gasoline engines in the farm home, including running sewing machines, ice-cream makers, sausage grinders and coffee grinders. A small one-horsepower engine was best for most household chores.

People wanting more advanced setups for household power could connect a larger engine to a long shaft in the basement, where all the household machines could be connected via pulleys and belts.

History Glance
1910s

Kato's own car

It was a big, bold and powerful machine, but the life of the Kato car was short-lived.

Louis Mayer of Mankato produced a series of cars in a downtown garage, including one of the first ever with a V-8 engine. His first, the Mayer Special, took its first jaunt down a Mankato road in 1907. Historians say it had advanced gear and suspension systems. Mayer would build several more models, including the innovative four-wheel-drive truck.

The run ended in 1915, however, amid a cloud of financial troubles. Mayer owed people money and didn't know how to market his cars. He scrapped his car building career after moving to Wisconsin.

Priest goes Over There

Pastor David Moran of the Catholic Church of St. Peter heeded the call to serve his country in World War I, entering the service as an Army chaplain in 1918. After serving in France, he was discharged one year later.

'Main Street' written in Mankato

Author Sinclair Lewis lodged in friend's Broad Street home to write novel

Nobel Prize winning author Sinclair Lewis wrote 'Main Street' while living in Mankato.

At the turn of the century, the Mankato area began to come into its own as a place not only for entertainment of the day, but as an incubator of creative thought and expression.

That atmosphere was emboldened by a temporary resident of Mankato who, while working on his craft here, achieved the area's greatest artistic success in the first quarter-century. It was in Mankato that novelist Sinclair Lewis wrote the novel "Main Street."

In the summer of 1919, novelist Sinclair Lewis moved to Mankato and lived in a house at 315 S. Broad St. owned by his friend, J.W. Schmitt.

Here, according to biographer John Koblas, author of "Sinclair Lewis, Home at Last," Lewis was able to focus on his writing and completed the books "Main Street" and "Free Air."

Lewis was a Sauk Centre native who became known as the area's resident free spirit. Much of the book's biting criticism of small town life was based on places and characters in Sauk Centre, although the novel had been written while Lewis lived in Mankato.

He wrote in the Schmitt home while that family, having been abroad, returned to live in a summer house on Lake Washington. The Schmitts allowed Lewis and his family to live in the Broad Street house rent free for two months.

Lewis loved the neighborhood, for both the relative anonymity he enjoyed (vs. Sauk Centre) and the friendliness of Mankato residents, although Mankato society's tolerance of Lewis' eccentricities was tested often.

He was notorious for crashing parties–though he was not at a loss for invitations–and sometimes he went so far for attention as to wear a hostess' dress. He and the Schmitts gathered weekly at Lake Washington, and Lewis also enjoyed the prestigious Point Pleasant resort, one of the area's finest resorts and one frequented by the well-to-do.

While in Mankato, he continued to make news. In July of 1919, Lewis addressed a large audience at the Mankato Teachers College, criticizing the state of popular fiction. In an essay for the *Atlantic Monthly*, he said, "I love America, but I don't like her," enraging many at this immediately postwar era.

But Lewis left Mankato at the end of summer, having successfully isolated himself in a small town where he wrote the bulk of "Main Street."

While the book is largely an indictment of Sauk Centre, it is nonetheless a composite of several towns in Minnesota. Mankato makes its mark as the hometown of its heroine, and–as Lewis explained in a letter to a Mankato friend before the novel's publication–"there are two descriptions of the loveliness and general agreeableness of Mankato, as contrasted with the flat prairie towns."

He signed a copy of the book "Free Air" for a friend in Mankato and wrote: "I wish I could send all of Mankato my new book–because I like Mankato just a little better than any other town in the world."

In 1930, Lewis was the first American awarded the Nobel Prize for Literature.

He returned to Mankato in 1947, while living in St. Paul, to gather new information for a book titled "The God Seeker." He refused a reporter's request for an interview at the time, in stark contrast to the publicity he craved three decades earlier.

Koblas wrote of Lewis' haggard cry to be left alone: "There was no longer any need to shock people; he was merely passing through Mankato, St. Paul, Minneapolis and Sauk Centre, researching a book he knew would never be a hit and taking a final look at places he had once, however briefly, called home."

Lewis died in 1951.

Front Street looking south, Mankato, MN

History Glance
1910s

Heavy lifting done here

Anything but buildings could be moved by William Page's Drayman and Furniture Mover business in the early part of the century.

Safes, pianos, boilers and engines could be relocated with Page's force of five two-horse teams and up-to-date equipment, the Free Press reported in 1915. The company also did light and heavy transporting of loads on a sturdy cart. Page, an early resident of North Mankato, began his Belgrade Avenue company in 1886.

Blue law for grocers

A multitude of grocers dotted Mankato during the era, stores such as Engwalson Bros. Dry Goods, U.S. Karmany's, Harry Alleman's, Otto Kammerer's Groceries, J.B. & D Richards Dry Goods, Slama Tea Co., Freshholtz Grocery, Patterson Mercantile, The Leader, and Grand Union Tea Co.

On June 21, 1915, Blue Earth County Attorney J.W. Schmitt sent a stern letter to Mankato grocers, ordering them to stop the practice of opening their shops for business on the Sabbath.

The flicker of entertainment

First movie theater in Mankato opened in 1906 with three more to follow

The Grand Theater opened in Mankato to local fanfare in 1913.

In 1900, traveling movies were introduced to the Mankato market. The first movie was believed to be shown in Mankato at 126 E. Jackson St. It was a traveling motion picture exhibit, and turnout was enthusiastic.

In 1906, the first theater in Mankato, the Majestic, was licensed in the 400 block of South Front Street, and in 1908 the Wonderland Theater opened.

Music at the Wonderland was provided by piano and drums, and movies shown were often along the lines of the Keystone comedies. The Wonderland, however, was a fairly uncomfortable place to spend much time. The chairs were old school chairs, there were no rest rooms and ventilation was poor.

That changed in 1913, when the Grand Theater was built, with the State Theater the following year.

The Grand had 1,000 seats, a stage, booth, canopy, lounge and restrooms, and all shows had at least a four-piece orchestra accompanying the movie.

The Grand's biggest draw was the weeklong run of "Birth of a Nation" in 1916. A symphony orchestra traveled with the picture and it remained the biggest selling feature at the Grand.

In 1908 moving pictures came to St. Peter when the Ludcke Brothers, William and Henry, built a theater on Main Street. They traveled to nearby Kasota, Madison Lake, Waterville and Kilkenny showing off the moving pictures.

The Ludcke Theater became the Opera House, where the St. Peter Association Band performed in shows combining motion pictures and music.

Another prime location for music and merriment was the Swan Lake Pavilion, built by Adolph Hermel, founder of Hermel Candy and Tobacco of Mankato, on his farm a mile north of Swan Lake.

Under the 100-by-58-foot pavilion, musicians such as Cliff Keyes and Whoopie John Wilfahrt played. The pavilion was torn down after 13 years in 1935, when the Depression contributed to low attendance.

A lack of funds threatened the St. Peter City Band in 1921, but the following year it was up and running with new members and monthly concerts at the Ludcke Theater.

A farmer is killed with ax, and his wife is acquitted

Hired hand convicted, but says she committed the actual murder

Life may have been hard and routine on the farm at the turn of the century, but it was not without its periods of scandal and intrigue.

One of the most famous, dramatic murder trials in local history featured a farmer killed with an ax, a hired hand with a shady background and accusations against the farmer's wife.

In the summer of 1909, after a 53-day search, the body of Holley Ledbeter was found buried near his barn on his farm just north of Mankato.

His hired hand, Frank Smith, was arrested for the murder. But Smith said it was Ledbeter's wife, Grace Ledbeter, who actually murdered her husband while he slept. Smith said she and he had discussed committing the crime, but that she carried out the murder. Smith said he only helped in disposing of the body.

Both Smith and Ledbeter were charged with first-degree murder. Authorities learned that Smith was actually Frank Lavendoski, who had a forgery conviction in Illinois.

After a lengthy, sensational trial, Smith was convicted of murder, while Ledbeter was acquitted. However, a second grand jury once again charged Ledbeter with murder, this time in the second-degree. A judge later threw out the charges, saying Ledbeter had already been tried for the crime.

Smith's life sentence was later reduced to 43 years and he was released on parole from Stillwater prison in 1939. Ledbeter stayed in Mankato for a short time, but reportedly left the state after receiving threatening messages.

History Glance
1910s

Check the fine print

In the early 1900s, teachers' duties and pay were put on a document a few pages long signed by school or town officials and the teacher.

In 1917, teacher Agnes Fitcher signed a seven-month contract for a salary of $40 a month. Town residents added language to the contract requiring her to kindle the fire every morning and serve as school custodian.

One 1914 contract got tough: too many older boys were misbehaving, marking and mutilating their desks. Teachers were forced to pay for the desks because of failing in their disciplinary duties.

Ring the bell

Before the turn of the century, women of the Presbyterian Church in Mankato raised $300 to buy a bell for the church steeple. For many years afterward, it served as the town bell, sounding alarms for emergencies as well as heralding joyous occasions such as Nov. 11, 1918 - the end of World War I.

Area churches grow, build

St. Peter Catholic church spent $2,500 on organ, $1,400 for furniture, pews

St. John's Episcopal Women's Guild members gathered in Mankato's Sibley Park for a picnic in July 1916 to fete the church's 50th anniversary.

By the turn of the century, many Mankato area churches had already existed for several decades.

Some had weathered two major 19th-century events, the Civil War and the bloody Minnesota Conflict between whites and Indians.

By 1900, most of the original church buildings were showing signs of wear, growing pains or both.

Typical of this early church expansionist era was the Catholic Church of St. Peter, where Ireland native the Rev. Patrick Carey arrived in 1908, ushering in a wave of parish growth.

During this period, the Sisters of St. Joseph came to St. Peter to teach in the parish's fledgling parochial school. In 1912, a new church was built. Records show that pews and furniture cost $1,400, the organ $2,500.

Churches kept in-house historical chronicles that were rife with esoteric details. The Swan Lake Lutheran Church historian noted that "in 1902 carpenter Lars Larson added a schoolroom and woodshed to the church. In the fall of 1931, the ladies decided to enlarge and remodel the woodshed for a kitchen. This time, Rudolf Borchert was to do the work."

At Evangelical Covenant Church in North Mankato, changes in worship services reflected a culture making the transition from Old World to new.

Evangelical pastor Joseph Johnson presided over the church's first services in English–they'd previously been in Swedish–and in Mankato, German and Norwegian Lutheran church members merged to form Bethlehem Lutheran Church in 1919.

Then, as now, churches relied upon members for support. But in the early part of the century, church officials' pleas for money were decidedly more codified.

At Trinity Lutheran in St. Peter in 1908, church elders developed a free will offering system that called for annual minimums: Men were to give $3, women $2. "Pew rents" also were a common way to bolster church coffers. For an annual fee of, say, $20, a family "owned" a pew for their personal use.

Among other things, the offerings went to pay church salaries. At the turn of the century at

Trinity, the pastor was paid $480 a year, the janitor $60. Organist Christine Borneman received an annual fee of $36.

During services one Sunday, Borneman couldn't get any sound to come from the organ. She got up and walked around to its side, where she came upon the source of the problem.

Two boys, paid 10 cents to pump the organ's bellows, had fallen asleep on the job.

A modern trend in churches has been to add recreational facilities and gymnasiums as a means of courting and keeping young members. But that concept locally was in full vigor in 1911, when SS. Peter and Paul's Catholic Church in Mankato built the Loyola Club in the downtown area.

The facility for young Catholic men featured a gym, bowling alley, billiard room and other recreational amenities designed to keep young men from straying from the church.

A news account heralded the new club this way: "It will afford them amusement of the right kind, where they will be under the eye of those who will guide them rightly."

A year earlier, a huge community turnout of all denominations feted the Rev. Robert Hughes of St. John's Catholic in Mankato.

The occasion was the 25th anniversary of his ordination, and the beloved cleric said he was considerably embarrassed to be lavished with so much praise.

The gala evening event featured eclectic entertainment, including a blind pianist and a humorist who parodied the foibles of Italian immigrants.

Far less gala was a 1922 fire that gutted St. John's Episcopal in Mankato. It was rebuilt in 1923, a year before Bethlehem Lutheran dedicated its new $45,000 building.

1910s

Farmers clubs popular

Farming at the turn of the century was grueling work, but rural families made a point of forging strong social ties and making the most of celebrations.

Farmers' clubs, where farm families met monthly for social, education and financial improvement, were prevalent in the early part of the century.

One of the oldest and most successful clubs in the nation was the Oshawa Township Farmers Club in Nicollet County, formed in 1913.

Farm groups also held major summer celebrations for their neighbors and city residents. A 1922 Free Press article recounted a 1922 Farm Bureau Picnic held at the Albert Jensen farm in Brighton Township of Nicollet County.

A 100-car caravan from St. Peter brought 500 city residents to the farm.

Women take larger roles in churches

Parishioners were dressed in their Sunday best circa 1911 at St. Paul's Evangelical Lutheran Church in Amboy.

After the turn of the century, women's roles in churches began to progress beyond the "auxiliary" functions that had limited females.

At Trinity Lutheran in St. Peter, church officials and pastors encouraged active participation in the church by laypeople.

In about 1910, Emma Langguth and several other church women took a 10-cent train ride to the Nicollet County village of Traverse–Pastor Luther Malmberg made the trip on his bicycle–to teach Sunday school to local children.

Those early inroads made by women set the course for full inclusion in church matters later on. In 1950, Trinity member Henry Benson proposed at a synod convention that women be allowed to serve as trustees at local congregations.

Mrs. Chester Johnson was elected to the Trinity church board. She's believed to be the first female in Augustana Synod history to be elected to such a post.

Johnson also was instrumental in getting a church library built that was open to the community and included art works and audiovisual equipment for lending.

Bethany starts as women's seminary

In 1999, Bethany Lutheran College in Mankato accommodated about 400 students, abounded with campus upgrades and stood poised to make the transition from a two-year to a four-year school.

But its origin began humbly in 1911, when a building to house a young women's seminary was erected on a hilltop overlooking downtown Mankato and the Minnesota River.

It served that function until 1927, when a small group of pastors and laymen bought the seminary and presented it to the Norwegian Lutheran Synod, which later became the Evangelical Lutheran Synod.

The purpose of the gift was to turn the facility into a school for young men and women. Bethany operated as a coeducational high school and junior college until 1969, when the high school portion closed.

Bethany Lutheran Theological Seminary became part of the campus in 1947 and by 1989 Bethany had 305 students from 16 states and two foreign countries.

A campus centerpiece, the S.C. Ylvisaker Fine Arts Center, was completed in 1990.

1920s

Sliced bread arrives

In the early 1920s, sliced bread came to Mankato.

Joe Ewalt was in his early teens and working for the Rindelaub Bakery, makers of BAMBY bread–short for Best American Bread Yet. The Rindelaubs bought the first bread-slicing machine in Mankato.

Eight to 10 people baked bread all night, and Ewalt has boyhood memories of running the loaves through the slicer and wrapping them for delivery.

'Messiah' performed

May Griffin, who arrived in Mankato from Boston in 1890, organized the largest musical event in Mankato's early history.

Griffin, a teacher at the Normal School, had often organized choirs and glee clubs and arranged for them to perform operas and oratorios along with musicians.

In 1922, Griffin organized 150 singers, four soloists and a full orchestra to perform Handel's "Messiah" in front of 1,700 people.

This performance is considered the precursor to the Mankato Symphony Orchestra, which would organize 18 years later.

City had competing hospitals

Catholic order took over municipal hospital in 1898; a Lutheran church later sponsored its own facility

The first St. Joseph's Hospital replaced the Tourtellotte Hospital on the city's north side and served Mankato for the entire first half of the 20th century.

Mankato, a no hospital town for its first 36 years, became a competitive medical market in 1906.

That's when Immanuel Hospital was built under the sponsorship of Immanuel Lutheran Church as an alternative to the Catholic St. Joseph's Hospital, opened in 1898 by the Sisters of the Sorrowful Mother.

The city asked the sisters for help after it opened a hospital following an $8,000 gift in 1888 by Col. John Tourtellotte, a former Mankato attorney and Civil War veteran. Operated by the city until 1897, the hospital was a major burden on the city treasury.

The order, with a $1,000 annual contract with the city in hand, whipped the operation into shape and had it in the black after one year. By 1898, the sisters had purchased a home on Sixth Street that was deemed a more suitable site than the Tourtellotte facility, which was on Fourth Avenue outside the city limits and without running water.

The sisters operated both hospitals until 1903, when the Tourtellotte facility was shut down. They completed construction of a new hospital just down the hill from the Sixth Street house. Named St. Joseph's Hospital, it was near the corner of Washington and Fifth streets.

The Lutherans set up Immanuel Hospital nearby, at Washington and Fourth streets. By 1912, an annex was built to increase capacity at Immanuel Hospital. St. Joseph's expanded the following year.

St. Peter asylum was state's first

The St. Peter Regional Treatment Center dates back to the city's early days.

Around 1866, the Legislature approved building the first state hospital for the insane, hoping the new facility would address the problem of the growing number of insane persons in county poor farms and jails.

The next problem was finding a location where the community was willing to deed 20 acres to the state.

To seal the deal, St. Peter leaders ultimately bought a 210-acre farm for $7,000 and gave it to the state. The new hospital was built for $295,000 from 1 million bricks taken from a quarry 400 feet from the site.

St. Peter State Hospital's first patient was accepted Dec. 6, 1866.

Overcrowding was a problem at the facility from the day it opened and continued over the years, according to staff.

By 1896, two other state hospitals had been added in Rochester and Fergus Falls.

In 1899, the Legislature established two asylums in Anoka and Hastings to relieve the overcrowding, provide housing and custodial protection for chronic cases, and let the three hospitals focus on care and treatment of the mentally ill.

Those patients, however, were replaced with old people "whose personal habits make their care irksome upon their relatives," according to an article by treatment staff in the *St. Peter Herald*.

In 1911, the Minnesota Security Hospital was built. Again, overcrowding became an immediate problem.

History Glance
1920s

North Kato paper starts

The only newspaper in North Mankato was the North Mankato Review, which enjoyed a 26-year run.

The Review was first published Sept. 8, 1921, by George Pusch. At the time its mainly national news was supplied by the Western Newspaper Union.

Nick Stemper bought the newspaper in the mid-1930s. When he died, his wife, Harriet, took over the business with Jack Kelly. The paper was sold to William Schuldt in 1944, who ran it until its final issue May 15, 1947.

Fire kills businessman

On Nov. 16, 1923, proprietor J.P. Durenberger succumbed to the same fire that claimed his harness shop at 528 S. Front St. The fire started when a furnace exploded. The estimated financial loss was $100,000.

Mary Lue's has a long history

Mary Lue's St. Peter Woolen Mill is one of the city's oldest industries, with four generations of the Brinker family employed there.

The woolen mill also is thought to be one of the first specializing in washing and carding wool in southern Minnesota.

The mill's history started in 1867, although its early ownership isn't completely clear. In 1880, the mill processed the wool of some 10,000 sheep in Nicollet and Le Sueur counties. In the early 1900s, John Charles Brinker took over the business.

He worked with his son, Charles Henry, who assumed ownership of the mill upon his death in 1931. In 1954, Charles Henry's son, Charles Eugene, bought the mill with his wife, Mary Lue.

Today, three of Charles and Mary Lue's children, Pat Johnson, Joel Brinker and Peggy Brinker, run the business.

The elder Brinker worked on an 1824 machine, while Charles Henry used an 1865 model, and Charles Eugene and his son, Joel, worked on a 1900 model.

At one point during World War II, part of the mill was used for carding of flax straw, making hemp for military rope.

The first mill was on North Front Street, later moving to 101 W. Broadway St. That mill building was torn down in 1960 for safety reasons. The machinery was moved to its present location, right next to where the old mill stood.

The store also expanded its small storefront in 1965 at Mary Lue's insistence. She believed more customers would come to the mill if more yarn was available. Additions were made to enlarge retail operations.

Today, products offered include needlepoint and crewel kits, looms, weaving supplies and knitting machines.

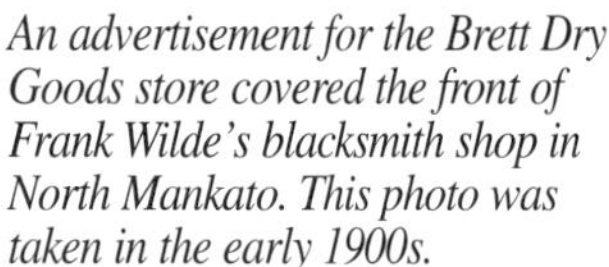

An advertisement for the Brett Dry Goods store covered the front of Frank Wilde's blacksmith shop in North Mankato. This photo was taken in the early 1900s.

The stock market crash of 1929 and ensuing years of the Great Depression brought hardship to the Mankato region, as well as the nation, but they also generated remarkable stories of perseverence and community spirit. Schools were hit hard. Wages dropped. Farmers struggled to keep their farms, burning corn for heat when they couldn't afford coal. They also faced drought in the early '30s.

But as one story here notes, "life was a mixture of good fortune and hard work."

With the arrival of World War II came the rationing of goods and other restrictions. Life was austere, but the community drew together to make do. Little went to waste. Parishioners routinely helped with repairs and maintenance work in their churches. But retail and grocery stores thrived. And local manufacturers produced key materials for the war effort–hemp for rope, generators for naval vessels and field hospitals, and tin cans. After the war, the region's higher education thrived.

These developments helped lay the foundation for the Mankato region's growth–and its future.

Chronicles of a Century

Part 2

1926 - 1950

Depression, war changed area retailing

Retailers struggled to get by during the '30s, prospered after the war

Brett's Department Store in downtown Mankato boasted a wide assortment of fabrics, lace, thread and other supplies for seamstresses.

The second quarter of the century brought tough times to southern Minnesota and to the nation. First came the Great Depression and then World War II.

During the Depression years of the 1930s, area businesses did what they could to help struggling families. The Mankato Chamber of Commerce played an active role in organizing a Mankato Community Chest in 1931. The fund was used to help care for impoverished families.

A similar fund was established in St. Peter and received support from businesses there, too.

On March 4, 1933, President Franklin D. Roosevelt closed banks nationwide to avoid irreparable damage from customer panic. Many people, fearing their financial institutions would become casualties of the Great Depression, had been rushing to empty their accounts. The exodus of funds carried some banks to the brink of collapse, and Roosevelt hoped the "bank holidays" would give people an opportunity to calm down.

Banks didn't begin to reopen until March 7, and many people were unable to cash paychecks. During the interim, countless area businesses extended credit to customers.

The Depression years were hard on retailers, too.

Paul Meyer said his father, Fred Meyer, started his appliance business in 1931, in the middle of the Depression.

To ensure that customers paid for refrigerators they purchased on installment plans from the store, the Meyers installed coin meters between the appliance and the outlet. To keep the refrigerator running, a customer had to feed quarters into the meter.

At the end of the month, Paul Meyer would empty the meters. The typical monthly payment for a Frigidaire was $4.50, he said.

Brett Taylor Jr., the 69-year-old great-grandson of George Brett, said his family's department store was forced to adjust. "During the Depression, we condensed everything," he said. "Every department became smaller."

The upper floor of the Brett's building, which had been devoted almost entirely to hats, was converted into doctors' offices during these austere years.

"We didn't have any money for advertising at the time, so the store employees put together a show," Taylor said. "They were called Brett's Entertainers, and they went around to small towns to promote the store." The show featured singing, dancing, skits and comic routines.

Many of the region's frugal residents preferred to make the most of their own clothes rather than pay for those manufactured by someone else during this rocky economic period. Stores such as Brett's catered to customers' wishes by stocking large inventories of fabric.

Sewing was a crucial skill. Only the well-to-do clientele could afford to hire the services of a tailor or seamstress to address their clothing needs.

In the late 1930s, Brett's began to offer ready-made clothing too. It did so mostly by leasing space inside the store to clothing manufacturers and taking a cut of their sales.

Building on its success in Mankato before the 1930s, Brett's had opened another store in Albert Lea just before the Depression hit. The Albert Lea store closed in 1934 and the fate of the Mankato store soon was also placed in question.

Taylor said, "The story I heard was that banks were calling in loans, and my grandmother had a $500 life insurance policy that she could borrow against. It saved the store in Mankato."

The loan proved to be a wise investment because sales rebounded dramatically during the 1940s.

The whole local economy swung into high gear when the nation entered World War II.

"I think most stores did pretty well during the war," Taylor said. "There was a shortage of goods, and whatever you got, you sold."

By 1940, Mankato's annual retail sales were estimated to have reached $13.4 million.

Business in downtown Mankato strengthened even more after the war drew to a close in 1945.

Longtime businessman Meyer said, "Downtown Mankato didn't really become a regional shopping mecca until right after the war."

Small grocery stores continued to rely mostly on neighbors for business. Former *Free Press* Editor Ken Berg wrote that in 1931 there were 44 retail grocers listed in Mankato's city directory. Most of them survived the Depression and saw business improve during the war years.

History Glance
1920s

Pay the cashier

Before the days of the modern cash register, some department stores devised systems that routed all transactions through a central cashier's office.

At Kresge's Department Store, invoices were placed in a basket attached by a hook to a moving track near the ceiling. The system would convey the bill, payment and change back and forth between the cashier and the sales attendant who was serving the customer at the checkout counter.

At Brett's Department Store, a pneumatic tube system was installed in the 1920s. It was used to shuttle tickets and money back and forth from sales counters and a cashier's office on the store's balcony level.

Brett Taylor Jr., whose father ran the store at the time, said the setup provided improved security and ensured that all transactions were handled by someone with sharp math skills.

But small grocery operations faced another threat. Larger grocery stores–supermarkets–had begun to arrive on the scene in Mankato. In 1933, the national Tea Co. opened its World's Fair Food Store on Front Street, employing more than 25 clerks.

An account in *The Free Press* said: "Modern developments in the store are the garden-like fruit and vegetable department, refrigerated meat department and arrangement of merchandise in open shelves illuminated by scientific arrangement of lighting equipment."

In 1942, Joe Ewalt bought the Steiner Bros. Grocery Store in the 300 block of North Front Street, following the death of its previous proprietor, his father-in-law.

Shortly after he assumed ownership, Ewalt was elected vice president of the Minnesota State Grocers Association. At the time, he says that 46 stores in Mankato and North Mankato were represented in the organization. "We had neighborhood stores in those days."

Ewalt and other grocers offered customers direct-to-the-door service. "We delivered more than half of the groceries we sold."

For the moment, neighborhood groceries were holding their ground.

Hotels were facing their own challenges.

In his Mankato history book called "A Bend in the River," Vern Lundin wrote that the decline of passenger train service and the growth of car travel marked the end of the big hotel business in Mankato. Most of the stately hotels of a previous era were being replaced by motels

These workers at the Martha Brandt Millinery Shop in Mankato created fanciful hats of all shapes and sizes.

Rationing felt in many ways during World War II

Consumption was limited by law, and recycling was required

Ration books and stamps were used to help conserve supplies of food and other essentials during World War II.

The typical resident could buy no more than three gallons of gas per week, one pound of coffee every five weeks, one pair of shoes every six months and five pounds of sugar every two months. The consumption of meat and canned goods was limited by means of coupons, as well.

Even restaurant goers felt the effect, according to *The Free Press*, which said, "The second cup of coffee virtually disappeared at local restaurants."

Little went to waste. Residents brought their used fats and oils to a collection site each month.

If you wanted to buy toothpaste, you had to turn in your old emptied tube first.

Concerns that there would be an inadequate supply of meat in the summer of 1943 prompted some river valley residents to consider wild game as an option. But hunting plans were hindered by a wartime restriction on ammunition: a maximum allocation of one box of shotgun shells per year.

The war effort had other impacts on the area's business community. Air raid drills brought the city to a halt on some occasions as it necessitated total blackouts of Mankato and North Mankato.

The end of the war proved somewhat disruptive, too. *The Free Press* described the events of Aug. 15, 1945: "By 7 p.m., Front Street was jammed with thousands of noisy celebrants. Those who did not hear of the news on their radios were brought out of their homes by the clamoring of whistles, bells, auto horns and firecrackers.

"Schoolboys had prepared confetti especially for the occasion, and mountains of the paper were thrown off buildings into the street below. Girls were embraced in public, and traffic was almost held to a standstill."

Corn was cheaper than coal

Cash was short in the '30s, but farmers at least had plenty of food to eat

Like everyone else in the nation, farmers were rocked by the Great Depression and World War II during the second quarter of the 1900s.

The stock market crash of 1929 and ensuing Depression hit many local farmers hard. Drought years in the early 1930s compounded the problem, driving many farmers to foreclosure.

For those who kept their farms, life was a mixture of good fortune and hard work.

Irvin Gunderson, a youngster on his parents' farm near Norseland during the Depression, said prices for farm commodities were painfully low.

"I remember some farmers were burning corn for heat because it was cheaper than buying coal."

But farmers had one advantage over city residents during the Depression, Gunderson said.

"At least farmers had their own meat to butcher. There was plenty of food available."

The average farm at the time was 160 acres, with virtually all farmers raising livestock. Corn, wheat, oats and pasture land dominated the rural landscape, with soybeans nearly nonexistent.

Horses were still the main power source on the farm, but tractor use was increasing significantly in the mid '30s.

Perhaps nothing symbolized the era more than threshing. Several neighbors usually jointly purchased a threshing machine and helped each other with the arduous job of removing the small grain seed from the hull.

The grain was cut and bundled in the field and left to dry for a week or so, and then brought to the farmyard for threshing.

Few farms had electricity, although some had small generator plants to run lights.

On May 11, 1935, Franklin D. Roosevelt created the Rural Electrification Administration, which brought electric lines to farmsites across Minnesota and America.

The local rural electric cooperative–now Frost BENCO Wells Electric–started two years later in 1937. Most farms were connected to power in the late '30s and early '40s.

While World War II took family members away and added stress to life on the farm, it also produced tremendous advances for agriculture.

Like everyone else in the country, farmers dealt with rationing of everything from tractors and rubber tires to sugar and other food items.

But government and private scientists, driven to improve food production during the war, made several dramatic discoveries that would launch the modern era of farming.

The production and use of synthetic chemicals in crop farming blossomed. In 1939, DDT was discovered for use to control pests (although it was later banned because of its effects on wildlife).

Chemical weed control also came on the scene, with the development of 2,4-D, one of the mainstays in weed control.

Also in the late 1930s, fertilizer improved with the introduction of anhydrous ammonia, solid urea and commercial granulation.

And the dairy industry–a mainstay of livestock farming at the time–was changed dramatically when a New Jersey dairy first used artificial insemination in 1938. The ability to breed higher producing milk cows through artificial insemination was one of the biggest advances ever in the dairy industry.

In 1948, scientists discovered B12 in the stomachs of livestock, leading to the creation and use of antibiotics for farm livestock. Antibiotics produced bigger, healthier animals.

When the war ended and the first half the century came to a close, farmers enjoyed the start of one of the most prosperous and promising times in agricultural history. The nation was strong and growing. Farmers enjoyed strong markets, better machinery and discoveries that improved their livestock and grain production.

During the first half of the century, virtually every farmer had livestock. This rural Mankato farm had a sizeable herd of cattle.

History Glance
1920s

The 'Eskimobile'

Between 1926 and 1932, Arthur Miller of Mankato manufactured something called an "Eskimobile," a machine similar to a snowmobile but with a fully enclosed cab big enough for several riders.

Miller's machine was similar to one used by the great Admiral Richard Byrd on his expeditions to the North Pole. Most of Miller's machines were used by mailmen and doctors who needed help reaching rural residents.

Selling for about $750, the Eskimobile worked like a Caterpillar tractor. It had 12-inch tracks on two sets of rear axles. The snow runners on the front of the machine were removable. In a 1971 Free Press article, Miller said he knew of several Eskimobiles around Minnesota in museums and antique shops.

St. Joseph's expands

St. Joseph's Hospital expanded again with a $200,000 addition.

Farming in the best, worst days

Lake Crystal couple got started in the field during the Depression

Earl and June Miner began farming on rented land on what is now hilltop North Mankato in 1934 and bought a farm in 1936 near Lake Crystal.

When Earl and June Miner got married and began farming in 1934, they were filled with optimism in spite of the Great Depression.

"We didn't know we were poor. Everybody was in the same boat," June said.

Added Earl: "We figured if we made enough to pay taxes and the debt on the farm and had a little left over, we were doing great."

The Miners first rented an 80-acre farm on what is now Hilltop North Mankato. In 1936 they bought a 160-acre farm near Lake Crystal that had been foreclosed on by a bank.

"The banks and insurance companies owned a lot of the farms then because people couldn't make it," Earl said. While many lost their farms following the stock market crash of '29, many farmers such as the Miners got their start by taking over foreclosed property.

Although they had no running water and no electricity, life on the farm during the Depression had its advantages.

"We always ate well," said Earl. "We had a garden and our chickens. We could butcher hogs or cattle."

But, added June, there wasn't much spending money either.

"You didn't spend anything on entertainment, you went over to the neighbors and played cards a lot. We never bought any new clothes; we were wearing our wedding suit and dress for years."

The Miners milked a dozen cows, raised 100 hogs a year and had about 300 chickens in the mid '30s. The chickens provided egg money and June raised extra money by butchering chickens on Saturdays, cooling them in well water and then taking them to Mankato to sell to regular customers.

"We'd sell them for 50 cents a piece instead of getting just 25 cents if they were live," June said.

While farm families struggled to stay solvent during the Depression, they faced new challenges and opportunities during World War II. Farm markets improved during the war, but rationing added new difficulties.

People had to go to a local rationing board for approval to buy tractors, cars, rubber tires or extra gasoline, sugar, butter and other items.

"The rationing board knew if you really needed something or if you just wanted it," Earl said. But for the most part, people lived miserly to help the war effort.

"People took it serious. They were very patriotic," Earl said.

Following the war, farmers had tremendous opportunity, Earl said.

"Anyone farming after the war made money. If you didn't, there was something wrong. It was a great time."

The Miners retired from farming in 1969, after seeing their share of prosperity and desperation on the farm.

"I always said we farmed in some of the best and some of the worst times," Earl said.

Hubbard Milling expands into livestock feed in 1928

Hubbard Milling Co. had been a major presence in Mankato since 1878, but it was 50 years after its birth that company officials made a momentous decision.

People must buy food not just for themselves but also for their animals. So in 1928, Hubbard Milling began producing Sunshine Concentrate for livestock producers, complementing the company's traditional flour milling.

That move to diversify from its five decade dependence on serving bakers, both commercial and in the home, led to massive growth for the company.

In 1946, the firm had a single flour mill and two feed plant operations, according to "Bend in the River: An illustrated History of Mankato-North Mankato." Its sales volume was $8 million.

By 1990, Hubbard was a multistate operation with $250 million in annual sales. Through acquisitions and internal product development, the company got into pet food production, turkey processing and a wide range of livestock feeds.

Businesses adapt to Depression

Mankato managed to avoid labor unrest mainly due to slow city growth

Immanuel Hospital, a Lutheran alternative to the Catholic St. Joseph's Hospital, operated at the corner of Washington and Fourth streets until the two hospitals merged in the late 1960s.

While the '20s in Mankato didn't necessarily roar, the Great Depression that followed didn't seem to hit with as much drama in southern Minnesota as it did elsewhere.

The violent labor unrest that struck Minneapolis and other large cities avoided Mankato. There were no reports of suddenly destitute speculators leaping from the windows of Front Street businesses or of folks relegated to selling pencils on downtown avenues.

Maybe it was because the area was not so prosperous in the decade leading up to the crash of 1929. The '20s weren't a good era for places heavily dependent on agriculture. The city's population grew by a modest 1,600 people, reaching 14,000 in the 1930 census.

Farmers were suffering from falling commodity prices, rising land values and increasing taxes.

And despite all of the attention on bank failures during the Depression, the agricultural struggles of the previous decade were largely responsible for 2,333 banks shutting down in the 1920s, according to "Land of the Giants," Don Larson's history of Minnesota business. For Minnesota, that was a greater number of bank failures than during the '30s.

Although businesses struggled in Mankato as in the rest of the world, other firms continued to form, adapt and even grow during the tough economic times of the Great Depression.

Purity Sausage Co. of Mankato replaced all of its equipment in 1931, just three years after the company was born, and purchased five new refrigerated delivery trucks from the Clement's auto dealership. Payroll grew to 15 in 1931, up from just three in 1928.

The Ramy Seed Co. was founded in 1932. There was even a resurrection in the local business community–the repeal of the 18th Amendment ended Prohibition in 1933 and brought the Bierbauer brewery, under new ownership, back to life with plans to produce 50,000 barrels of brew a year.

The Carney cement company, feeling the competition from the rapidly spreading Portland cement plants, began producing "rock wool" in 1939 in a new plant on the north side of town. Created by heating and blowing waste rock from local quarries, the cotton-like material was sold as insulation.

That same year, the Mankato Soybean Products company opened its mill, turning soybeans into meal and oil.

And in November 1941, the Continental Can Co. was constructing a new plant in Mankato. A month later Japan would attack Pearl Harbor and command control of much of the world's tin-producing regions.

The onset of World War II brought both challenges and opportunities to Mankato business and industry.

Minnesota business lost 300,000 workers to military service during the early years of the war, according to Larson's book. Others left for high-paying defense jobs in Alaska and on the West Coast.

Firms relying on traveling salesmen to move their goods were partially grounded by gas rationing. Special gas rations, allowing up to 8,600 miles of yearly travel, were provided to only 200 of Mankato's estimated 400-600 salesmen in 1943.

War restrictions on building in nondefense zones caused the value of building permits to drop 81 percent in 1942, according to a *Free Press* article.

But the war may have increased the number of new workers coming into the city. Only 29 houses and apartments were available for rent in Mankato in January of 1943, down from more than 100 the previous October.

"Increased payrolls at the Mankato Ordnance Pool, the Little Giant Co., Kato Engineering and Armour's accounts for the influx of population in Mankato, according to E.V. Nyquist, secretary of the Chamber," the *Free Press* reported.

Little Giant trip hammers were in big demand at machine shops during the war, and government contracts often specified "Little Giant or equal," according to Vern Lundin's "At the Bend of the River." Mankato Ordnance Pool, renamed MICO after the war, produced brakes for military equipment.

Kato Engineering supplied generators for naval vessels, field hospitals, army field headquarters and other military units.

Hemp mills in Lake Crystal and Mapleton provided the raw material to produce rope for the military.

Continental Can announced it was using a new method of manufacturing cans which used less tin. The *Free Press* saw the process as another example of how the nation's companies have "outflanked Japanese control of most the world's tin and have written another chapter in the story of American industrial foresight and ingenuity."

Dairies dominated town in '30s

Nicollet County laid claim to 13 dairies, many brands of butter and products

The Wettergren and Sons Dairy was the last milk-processing facility in Nicollet County when it closed its doors after being sold to Cloverleaf Dairy of Minneapolis in 1973. Clarence A. Wettergren (in truck) started the dairy with help from his sons (left to right) Bill, Bud and Bob.

Back then, the milkman knew what you needed for dairy products and placed it in your icebox while you were still sleeping.

Those were the days that spanned into the years from 1925 to 1950, when Nicollet County laid claim to 13 creameries.

Those were the days of "Cow Street."

That's what Front Street in St. Peter was called, but not because of the dairies along it.

The street was dubbed so because of the local people from the south end of town and along the Minnesota River who herded their cows north on Cow Street to a 25-acre pasture where Veterans Park is today.

Each day, those cows passed the St. Peter Creamery, the Wettergren and Sons Dairy and the Borsch Dairy as they made their way to Madison Street and over Minnesota Avenue.

Soren Smidt bought the St. Peter Creamery in May 1930. A report of the day touts the creamery as dispensing 5,000 butterfat checks a month.

"All going out to the local farming community to help fight off the threat of low grain prices and the justifiable fear that there is going to be a long, long road to the Tipperary of farm relief," it said.

Smidt produced the "Minnesota Valley" brand of butter, complete with a logo depicting a typical hut of early county settlers, a stockade and early Indians.

Stan Davis bought the St. Peter Creamery during World War II, changing its focus from buying cream to separating whole milk and later drying milk into powder. The business grew into the international Davisco Co. now in Le Sueur.

Wettergren and Sons Dairy was started by Clarence A. Wettergren in Traverse in 1930. On his first day of business, Wettergren bottled 36 quarts of milk, selling half of it door-to-door.

The second day, he sold the remaining 18 quarts, plus another 36 quarts. As business grew, the dairy moved to Front Street in 1935. Customers included local stores, schools, hospital and Gustavus Adolphus College.

Wettergren's sons, Bill, Bud and Bob, delivered milk before they went to school each day.

"We started early in the morning and would have half a day's work in before we even went to school," said Bob Wettergren, of St. Peter. "That's why we'd fall asleep."

Over the years, several smaller dairies–including the small Borsch Dairy, St. Peter Milk Co., Mortensen Dairy, Skoog Dairy and the Walter Olson dairy–sold out to the Wettergrens. When it was sold to Cloverleaf Dairy of Minneapolis in 1973, it had more than 500 customers.

The Model Dairy opened a $25,000 plant on Third and Nassau streets in 1930, an extension of the Model Dairy already operating in Mankato. The dairy didn't offer home delivery, but locals could purchase milk and butter at the creamery.

It employed 30 people in 1930, processing 750,000 pounds of butter a year and 100 gallons of ice cream daily.

In North Mankato, Earl and Marie Smith and Merrill and Miriam Claridge opened Purity Dairies on Nicollet Avenue in 1927. The 15-employee dairy processed milk, butter and cottage cheese.

In 1936, Claridge created Marigold Dairies. Soon after, he built a $60,000 plant on Belgrade Avenue and Ball Street and employed 25, with an annual payroll of $29,000. The employees included four office and eight plant workers and 13 salesmen-drivers.

The dairy was one of the largest employers in North Mankato from 1940 to 1965, with up to 80 employees. Marigold's products included milk, cream, butter, Dario orangeade, cottage cheese, ice cream, sherbets, chocolate milk and frozen strawberries.

A headline on a 1937 news report declared "Dairy workers wear mittens even in July."

"Inside the hardening room, hoarfrost hangs white and thick around the more than one-half mile of one and one-half inch pipe, which coils beneath the ceiling and around the walls of the room. The icy cold congeals the breath and sends shivers through anyone not dressed for a wintry atmosphere."

History Glance
1920s

Circus in St. Peter

The circus came to town in St. Peter - and stayed.

The Schell Bros. Circus, owned by Mr. and Mrs. George Engesser, was thought to be the second largest motorized circus in the country around 1930. It included one elephant, 20 truck loads of equipment, Leo the Lion and a small menagerie. All told, its equipment was valued at $65,000.

The circus came about when a traveling vaudeville troupe came to St. Peter. Short a piano player, George Engesser, a local boy who worked at Danielson's Music Store, was recruited to play with the group.

Engesser went on to vaudeville for a couple of years, where he and his wife started an "Ole Show" featuring Swedish comedy. The couple returned to St. Peter in 1925 to start Zellmar Bros. Circus, changing the name to Schell Bros. in 1927.

Her Valley ran Deep into hearts

Maud Hart-Lovelace based Betsy-Tacy series on her own and daughters' lives

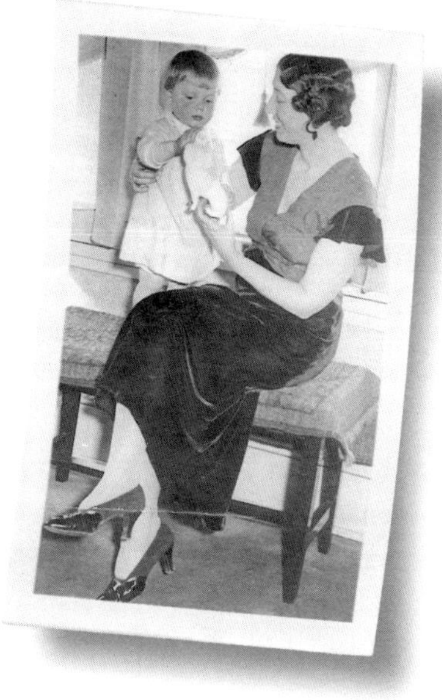

Maud Hart-Lovelace with her daughter Merian in 1932. Much of Merian's later exploits in life inspired the plots of Lovelace's Betsy-Tacy books.

As Mankato entered the 20th century, much of its cultural identity was shaped by the activities in new buildings, clubs and organizations. Its most far reaching and famous artist, however, was darting about town playing with her friends.

Mankato native Maud Hart-Lovelace would in the mid-20th century write a series of children's books that would have lasting effect into the next century, and one that certainly put Deep Valley–her storybook name for Mankato–on the map of many a young imagination.

Lovelace, born in 1892, was the author of the Betsy-Tacy series of children's books, semiautobiographical stories about Lovelace and her childhood friends and their adventures in Mankato.

Lovelace began writing in a maple tree in her backyard as a child and many of her rhymes made it into the local newspaper.

After her high school days, Hart wrote short stories while attending the University of Minnesota, selling her first, "Number Eight," while visiting a grandmother in California. She married Delos Lovelace in 1917 and when he returned from World War I, she began writing novels.

In 1921, they moved to Manhattan and 10 years later a daughter, Merian, was born.

The Betsy-Tacy books grew out of Maud Hart-Lovelace's storytelling to her daughter. Her stories of her childhood were so well-received by her daughter that Lovelace apparently decided she had a good book if she could collect the stories on paper.

By then, she had already written historical works such as "Early Candlelight," "Black Angels," and "The Charming Sally."

The first piece, "Betsy-Tacy," drew a good response and publishers Thomas Y. Crowell Co. allowed the follow-up "Betsy-Tacy and Tib." The series was under way, interrupted occasionally for non-Betsy books such as 1950's "The Tune Is in the Tree" and 1952's "The Trees Kneel At Christmas." Hart-Lovelace wrote 13 Betsy-Tacy related books in all.

Merian graduated from high school in 1948, the year her mom published "Betsy and Joe," in which the heroine graduated from Deep Valley High.

Betsy's adventures followed Merian's: when in 1948 Merian moved to Smith College, Lovelace began writing college adventures for Betsy's friend Carney. When Merian visited Europe, Lovelace wrote "Betsy and the Great World," and "Betsy's Wedding" was published shortly after Merian wed a New York magazine editor.

The Lovelaces moved to California in 1954, where Delos wrote fiction and Lovelace continued the series. The author relied on a good memory, as well as diaries and letters, to help her bring the past to life for a growing number of readers.

At that point, the fascination with her stories and their settings began drawing the curious to Mankato to visit old houses in the Lincoln Park neighborhood.

Lovelace died in 1980, the year the Minnesota Regional Valley Library dedicated a mural in the Lovelace Wing depicting Mankato's various points of significance.

In 1990, Lona Falenczykowski and 11 other Mankatoans established the Betsy-Tacy Society, with a national membership of more than 1,200. In July 1997, visitors from around the country converged on Mankato in honor of what would have been the 100th anniversary of Betsy's fifth birthday, visiting various Mankato landmarks linked to the Betsy-Tacy stories.

Such landmarks include the society-owned 332 Center St. childhood home of Tacy (actually Frances Kenney) and the site of a small bench on which Hart and friends sat as children.

A new bench was eventually built and a plaque on it reads "To honor Maud Hart-Lovelace, who here began the childhood daydreams that one day would be our window to the past."

1930s

What's a pizza?

Paul Meyer, a longtime Mankato businessman, recalls there was quite a stir in town when Pete's Pizza Parlor opened in the late 1930s.

"Everyone wondered what the heck a pizza was."

Roosevelt opens

Roosevelt Elementary, built in 1927, has only had three principals since it opened: Beatrice Marks from 1927 to 1959, Donald Hager from 1959 to 1983 and Joel Botten from 1983 to the present. Roosevelt and Franklin are two existing Mankato Area Public Schools built in the late 1920s.

North Mankato's first cop car came in the 1930s

After a two-year squabble, the North Mankato Police Department purchased a 1932 Essex six-coach automobile as a mobile police unit. The chief at the time had to use police funds raised through special events to buy the truck. The council agreed, however, to supply gas and oil for the vehicle.

Higher ed boomed after war

Teachers, like others, suffered financially during the Depression years

A World War II training program created a housing shortage at Gustavus Adolphus College in St. Peter. Trailers were moved to campus to house young trainees and their families.

Oshawa teacher Alice Poncin didn't reveal her wages in her writings, but she describes them as so low she couldn't afford to eat.

The Depression hit schools hard: families couldn't afford tuition, and schools–whether supported by taxes, churches or tuition–couldn't afford building repairs or decent wages.

Poncin complained so many women were willing to teach to earn extra money that wages were dropping. However, she doesn't say whether these women were married or if they were delaying marriage in order to support their parents, brothers and sisters.

In Edna Snyder's writings, she made it clear school officials didn't think highly of working married women, even during the Depression.

The Oshawa teacher taught successfully for a few years in her district. When school officials learned she planned to marry, they put a clause in her contract that she would be fired if she married during the school year.

The gender gap in salaries continued in the following decade: in 1944, salaries in Blue Earth County ranged from $179 to $257 for men and $127 to $156 for women.

As times improved, so did conditions in schools. Yet rural schools couldn't keep up with the accommodations offered in city schools. A Ceresco Township school, for example, proudly announced the installation of electricity in 1941.

Around the same time, a North Mankato school was installing a fancy broadcast system that allowed radio reception for educational broadcasts and two-way communication between classrooms and the office.

The education system also was improving and teaching standards were becoming more stringent. In 1930, the Mankato Teachers College offered its first full four-year curriculum and entrants were required to have a high school diploma for admission.

World War II also affected schools.

Mankato's high school burned in a spectacular fire in July 1941, but the war prevented school officials from rebuilding. Supplies were greatly restricted at the time.

Gustavus Adolphus College joined a program during the war that boosted enrollment as they trained young men for the Navy, Marines and Coast Guard. (Some 420 men enrolled in the two years it was offered.)

When the war ended, post-secondary institutions boomed. Lawmakers pumped money into vocational schools to train men for careers. The Mankato Area Vocational School was established in 1945.

The Mankato Teachers College's mission began to evolve with more of a focus on arts and sciences. Returning vets weren't only interested in teaching careers; they wanted jobs in business and science.

Meanwhile, small schools were beginning to consolidate into larger districts. State funding was tied to enrollment, so more students translated into more money. Additionally, city schools could offer industrial arts, hot lunch and other unique programs. These were attractive to many rural families, yet some fought the end of the country school.

Gustavus takes role in naval training

World War II took men who normally would have been in jobs or colleges and put them in military service. Rosie the Riveter helped on the job front, but colleges were looking for ways to maintain healthy enrollments.

Gustavus Adolphus College in St. Peter found a way to boost its numbers by participating in the Naval College Training program from July 1943 to October 1945. The so-called V-12 program trained seamen for the Navy, Marines and Coast Guard. Gustavus was the only college reserve program to also train for the Marine Corps.

Regular students had to adjust to the surge of trainees who came to St. Peter. The program did well enough to cause a campuswide housing shortage. Trailers were hauled to St. Peter to provide housing for young men and their families. An eating area had to be added to Uhler Hall.

In all, 420 young men entered the program, sharing academic classes with their civilian counterparts.

To accommodate training needs, some professors volunteered to teach outside of their subject areas.

A military ship was named after the college program: the S.S. Gustavus Victory became the 24th ship sponsored by a college.

After the war, colleges and universities received a boost from federal programs that provided money to returning veterans to get an education.

The G.I. Bill, as it is commonly called, helped vets pay for tuition and books.

Printer stumbled into a business that would make him millions

With $300, Bill Carlson started one of area's biggest businesses

Bill Carlson's first printing press is housed at the Blue Earth County Historical Society.

During its first month of business in 1948, Carlson Letter Service had $25 in total sales. Today, Carlson Craft, part of Taylor Corp., processes between 8,000 and 10,000 printing jobs daily, employs about 2,200 and earns more than $100 million in annual sales.

Founder Bill Carlson says he stumbled into the printing business. Following his discharge from the Army in 1945, Carlson knew he wanted to be his own boss, but he wasn't sure what kind of business to pursue.

He considered starting a diaper service, opening an appliance store, selling packaged sandwiches or operating a small lodging house.

The idea of getting into the printing business came from a U.S. Commerce Department publication: Business Ideas for Returning Servicemen.

"No one told me that it was impossible to start a business with only $300, so we went ahead and did it," Carlson told *The Free Press* for an article celebrating the company's 50th anniversary.

The couple sent out its first flier to about 50 local businesses. For $1.15, they offered to mimeograph 100 letters and deliver each order to the customer's door.

Carlson continued to work another job as an accountant at Swanson's Wallpaper and Paint for several months before quitting to devote his attention to printing.

The Carlsons soon acquired a small hand-operated printing press and began to print customized napkins, stationery and wedding invitations.

Carlson decided to sell his products wholesale–rather than retail–so he could concentrate on the business of printing. As a wholesaler, Carlson was able to access more markets, and business began to snowball.

Fire in 1941 destroyed school; war delayed its reconstruction

Eventually what is now Mankato West was built in a swampy area

Mankato's high school was destroyed by fire in 1941. It was at Hickory and South Fifth streets.

The burning of Mankato's High School at Hickory and South Fifth in 1941 should have been no surprise: a state fire marshal had condemned the building in 1939.

School officials, however, hoped a few repairs would correct the problem.

The day after summer session was dismissed, students returned to pick up report cards from the building, which also was serving as a polling place for school elections.

Fire broke out and the building was destroyed.

Band director Karl Aaberg raced into the blinding smoke to save several band instruments. A few trophies, some paperwork and the election ballots were also salvaged.

Still, many of the district's records and mementos were lost.

Some parents were actually relieved because the school was in such bad shape.

But hopes for quick reconstruction were dashed by World War II because building supplies were restricted.

The district had to shuffle students around for 10 years: high school students went to Lincoln junior high, junior high students went to Franklin and many Franklin students went to the Union School.

When discussions about the new high school began, the debate quickly heated up.

Planners chose an area known as the "slough" for construction, also known as Memorial Field.

Opponents didn't want the school built in a wetland, and it took three citywide votes before the $795,000 bond issue passed.

Mankato West High School opened in 1951 and in two decades, it was clear the school wouldn't be large enough.

Mankato East High School opened in 1973.

Streetcars are driven out of city

Increased desire for automobiles ends demand for streetcars in Mankato

The Coy Cab Co. operated buses and taxi cabs that ran between Mankato and North Mankato and on long-distance routes as far away as Omaha and Chicago in the 1930s and 1940s.

In the local battle between automobiles and streetcars, the second quarter of the 20th century saw automobiles emerge the clear winner.

Cars and car dealerships peppered the area landscape, including the addition in 1933 of the Ford dealership and an International Harvester dealership in 1935.

More autos, however, meant more auto problems.

In 1948, Mankato Police Chief E.A. VanThuyne urged automobile drivers to be cautious when driving, as the previous year saw the most car crashes ever to that point. There were 525 auto crashes that injured 98 people and killed one.

VanThuyne urged city officials to construct a bypass route to take traffic congestion away from the city's business district. He suggested that route run through North Mankato.

The emergence of the automobile spawned offshoots such as buses and taxi cabs.

In the 1930s, Ed and Don Wold purchased the Mankato City Lines bus company and its one bus. In 1936, the bus hauled 36,000 passengers at 6 cents apiece on a single route between Sibley Park and Front Street. The company served Mankato and North Mankato for more than 36 years before selling its operations to the city.

Gas was cheap. Motorists could get five gallons of gas for 67 cents, a vehicle overhaul for about $25 and a new car for $580.

Streetcars finally died in 1930 when, after changing hands three times, the company that started out as the Mankato Traction Co. was abandoned. Between 1922 and 1930, the company operated at increasing losses as automobiles began to dominate.

Air travel began to take off in the '20s and '30s, with Mankato getting its first airport in 1928. That first year, four pilots used the airport, which was near Mankato State Teachers College. Ten years later, 49 pilots used it. Prior to that, local pilots used open fields or roadways to take off and land planes. Among those was Gust Imm, a Mankato aviator who in 1926 flew from Minneapolis to Mankato in 55 minutes, landing at the top of Windmiller Hill at the end of Rhine Street.

The boom years for local aviation came with World War II, when Uncle Sam used the Mankato airport to teach youngsters to fly planes in combat.

Trains also chugged away in the second quarter of the century.

In 1936, Chicago and North Western's "Famous 400" arrived in Mankato, bringing "luxury" train travel to the area for the first time. The 400, named for the number of minutes the trip took, offered air conditioning and took just over six hours to travel from Mankato to Chicago.

Mankatoans paid a mere $18.85 to ride the train to Chicago, and just $13.11 to Milwaukee. Residents would lament the 400's demise 30 years later when lack of ridership forced the company to stop all passenger routes from Mankato.

Prior to that, Mankato delighted in a new freighthouse for the Milwaukee Road, although the *Mankato Free Press* had this to say about the new facility:

"It's a classy place all right. It reeks with class. That is, it reeks with class for what it's meant to be–a freighthouse. But whoever heard of a classy freighthouse? A freighthouse is no place for fussy office girls. Nor is it a place for the 'persnickety' office man. It's a place where you put your feet on the desks, throw your cigarettes on the floor and spit at the belly stove. But you can't even cuss in comfort in the remodeled Milwaukee Road freighthouse at the foot of Hickory Street."

This is a shot of St. Peter's Minnesota Avenue believed to have been taken during the 1930s or 1940s.

History Glance
1930s

Homemade bratwurst

SS. Peter and Paul's Catholic Church parishioners in the 1930s took a made-from-scratch approach to their annual community bratwurst suppers.

Each December, men and women of the Mankato church went to the George Sieberg farm near Eagle Lake, where they slaughtered and butchered six or seven hogs, ground the meat, and made it into sausage.

Its final note

In 1931, the Mankato Opera House was torn down to make room for the Holt Motor Company.

But in its prime, the Mankato Opera House brought stage stars, boxers and wrestlers to the city.

It had been built in 1872 as Harmonia Hall on the 200 block of South Second Street. A fire in 1882 destroyed it, but it was rebuilt several months later as the Mankato Opera House.

Brown saw airport take wing

Early aviator became interested in flying because he hated to drive a car

Mankatoan Dean Brown flew airplanes for nearly 70 years, including this one in the 1940's.

In 1928, when the first local aviation enthusiasts built an airport near what is now Minnesota State University, Dean Brown was learning how to fly.

A few years later, when the U.S. Navy was using the airport to train combat pilots, Brown was flying alongside them.

And in the early 1990s, 65 years after his first solo flight, Brown was still logging air time.

"I didn't like to drive. Still don't," Brown said. "I used it as transportation. It got to be very commonplace for me."

At 94, Brown is probably one of the oldest living local residents who remembers the early days of aviation in Mankato.

Before the area's first airport was built, he said, aviators used a cornfield west of town on the Seppman farm to take off and land. Those were the days when flight was nothing more than a curiosity to most people. Local newspapers from the early 1900s contained articles about daring pilots who flew from Minneapolis to Mankato.

"In those days," Brown said, "we flew out of any field that was open."

The old planes weren't technologically complex.

"They didn't even have airspeed [gauges] on the first ones," he said. "You just had to look out the window."

Soon a handful of local pilots was navigating the skies, prompting the need for a better airport. In 1928, at a cost of about $7,000, a new cornfield was chosen near Mankato Teachers College on a dairy farm owned by Bob Rasmussen. Lawrence Sohler built the airport and constructed a hangar for pilots to park planes.

"It was just a hangar with an office in the corner," Brown said.

He recalls his first solo in 1934, where he made a few trips around the airport before landing. He was nervous, he said.

"It was dangerous. A lotta people got killed monkeying with these things."

Four years later, Brown bought his first airplane, a Taylorcraft. It would be the first of some 15 planes Brown would own before turning in his wings.

Brown bought that plane just a few years before the event that he says gave aviation its biggest boost ever: World War II.

"The war taught thousands of kids to fly," Brown said. "And that was the real beginning of aviation."

Hundreds of local boys were trained for war at the Mankato airport. But Brown, who was not a military pilot, said that training didn't equate to busy skies when the boys came home. The horrors of war, he said, grounded many of those pilots.

Brown, who owned the Buick dealership in Mankato, continued to fly. And better planes continued to be built.

Of the many planes he flew, his favorite was the Beechcraft Bonanza, an aircraft that came out in the 1960s that revolutionized the private plane. The Bonanza zoomed at a top speed of 180 mph, much faster than any other single-engine plane at the time.

Another flight revolution was when the Piper airplane company built the Cub, an affordable plane that for many early pilots was the first plane they owned.

Brown logged thousands of hours flying all over the country, including such places as New York, California and Florida.

"I flew just to fly," he said.

His skills progressed over the years until flying became easy. But it was never simple. Especially when he used advanced piloting skills to navigate at night or in poor weather.

"It got to be quite a job, flying," Brown said. "It's not as trivial as it looks."

At 94, Dean Brown was proud to say he stopped flying airplanes only a few years ago. He was alive before Mankato had an airport and lived through virtually every phase of Mankato's aviation history.

History Glance
1930s

Cobbler gets started

At the height of the Depression, Miles Lunak, a longtime fixture in the city of St. Peter, started his shoe repair business in 1931.

Lunak repaired shoes, boots binder canvasses, luggage, athletic equipment and zippers on women's corsets for years, according to the St. Peter Herald.

He later was thought to be the oldest self-employed businessman in St. Peter, the paper said.

Brickyard closes

When William E. Stewart closed his Mankato Brick and Tile Co. in 1935, it marked the end of an era.

By 1892, some 15 brickyards in the Mankato and North Mankato area were manufacturing more than 12 million bricks. Stewart's company was the last brickyard to be opened, later falling victim to the Depression.

The company used alluvial clay mined from behind the Stewart home at 733 Range St. for its bricks, leaving behind the depression still evident in North Mankato's Wheeler Park.

Fishing pals reel in big one

Duo made improved fishing reel from alarm clock, homemade parts

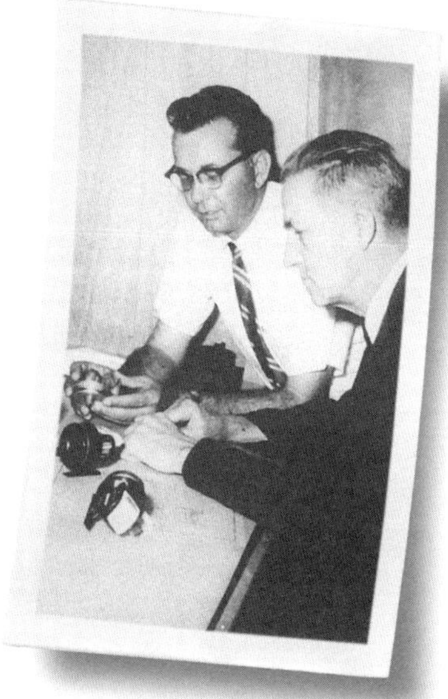

Lloyd Johnson (right) was the inventor of the Johnson fishing reel, a product that became world famous and was the key to the creation of Denison-Johnson Inc., a major employer in Mankato beginning in 1950. Also pictured is chief engineer Gene Menne.

Mankato has a long history in reel making, all starting with high hopes for an improved fishing reel.

In 1949, Lloyd Johnson and his fishing partner, Warren Denison, began assembling the first Johnson reels in Johnson's West Mankato basement. The pair decided that "there must be a better way to fish" and set about designing a reel that would cast easily and accurately without backlash.

Fifty years later, the company has become a world leader in marketing and distribution of fishing, camping, diving and marine products.

Using an old alarm clock casing and some hand-forged parts, Johnson and Denison assembled their first reel, using it and showing it to friends and at fishing shows.

It wasn't long before they realized they had a hit on their hands. In 1950, they turned out 1,000 "sidewinder" spincast reels, and the company was off and running.

With rapid consumer acceptance, the company moved from the Johnson basement to a garage and, later, to the first permanent factory building at 720 Minneopa Road.

The entire production, sales and management force in the early days of the company consisted of Johnson and Denison and their wives.

In 1955 the company introduced the first Model 100 Century reel. The reel represented the company's departure from what were known as "the old sidewinders," early reels in which the monofilament line was delivered out of the side of the reel instead of through the front cover. The company quit producing the "sidewinders" in about 1959.

Development of the Century reel led to a whole new range of ideas, and the company quickly brought out a larger version of the Century, called the Citation, and a new reel called the Centennial, so named because it was produced first in 1958, the year of Minnesota's centennial observance. Acceptance of the reels throughout North America was excellent.

Between 1958 and 1963, Johnson Reels Inc. dove into production of fishing rods to go with the reels. The company bought and operated the Philipson company in Denver, but later sold it back to its original owner.

Electronics business had its timing right

Kato Engineering Co. had already been in business for more than a decade when World War II broke out.

With the military demand for power equipment during the war, business prospered. Electrical generators were ordered for naval vessels, field hospitals, the Signal Corps and the Sea Bees.

Already, at the end of the 1930s, the company was awarded government contracts to build generators for the Army Air Force.

The company was established in 1926 by L.A. Wilkinson and E.J. Jenson in Mankato. Two years later, Cecil Jones joined the company at 727 S. Front St.

During the Depression, Jones and several others purchased stock in the company. He became its president in 1934.

It was Jones who designed an electrical device that led to the company's initial growth. That device–a rotary converter dubbed the "Kato Converter"–changed DC to AC power. It was used on farms to run AC appliances such as radios and electric irons on DC storage batteries.

Another of Kato Engineering's products at that time was an eliminator that replaced "B" batteries in DC radios. The company's product line was expanded with small engine driven AC generators.

Kato Engineering became known for its ability to build one-of-a-kind machines, developing a niche for special designs and quantities other manufacturers weren't interested in making.

In 1945, Kato Engineering employed 497. When sales declined after the war, the work force was reduced to about 150. Kato gradually broke into the commercial and industrial market for power generation.

History Glance
1940s

Jones starts with three employees

Organized in 1942 by C. H. Jones, who worked for Kato Engineering, Jones Metal Products originally designed and produced sheet metal items for Kato generators. The staff consisted of Jones and two sheet metal workers.

Kept busy during World War II supplying Kato's needs for the much-in-demand generators used by the military, Jones Metal Products expanded after the war. The company provided heating, air-conditioning and ventilation materials for building contractors and individual homeowners.

Soon, the company was winning a regular group of industrial customers who needed specific metal products fabricated. Kato Engineering remained a prized customer but was joined by companies like 3M, Honeymead, Caterpillar and numerous others.

Churches, members make it through the Depression

A church's ledger shows a total of 10 cents in its collection one Sunday

The Rev. Alphonse Schladweiler, flanked by altar boys, broke ground in July 1949 for the new Holy Rosary Catholic Church in North Mankato.

The Depression and World War II formed a one-two punch on U.S. society during 1926-1950 and churches suffered accordingly.

Small but significant upgrades–in 1927 electric lights were installed at Immanuel Lutheran in Courtland–paled alongside the nation's looming hard times.

In the early 1930s, the Depression made money scarce for churches as parishioners had all they could do just to keep their families solvent.

Rather than hire contractors, church repairs were routinely done by parishioners, when repairs could be afforded.

A Depression era ledger from the Methodist Church in Mankato bore evidence of flagging revenues and attendance. One Sunday, five worshippers showed up and put 10 cents in the collection basket. The next Sunday was better, relatively speaking. The 14 people who attended contributed 33 cents.

The penury that churches were forced to endure also made it difficult to retain clergymen.

St. John's Episcopal in Mankato was without a rector from 1929 to 1932. Several clergy tried to fill the gap, but parish life suffered and attendance on Sundays often fell below 30. In summer, it wasn't uncommon for services to be canceled for lack of worshippers. But churches began to rebound in the mid-1930s, and many experienced a steady period of growth. New denominations also came to the fore.

In 1938, the Mankato congregation of Jehovah's Witnesses held its first meeting in a member's apartment on North Front Street. A year later, the group rented a room above Mahowald's hardware store. Several years later, the growing congregation built a Kingdom Hall on Third Avenue.

In 1941, St. John's Episcopal marked its 75th anniversary with a daylong fete that climaxed with a parish dinner. Also that year, a Minneapolis crusader against vice expressed his disappointment with the Mankato area for not being more cooperative against the forces of evil.

Only about 100 people showed up at Belgrade Avenue Methodist Church in North Mankato to hear the Rev. J. Henry Soltau harangue against sin.

"It's difficult to make headway in Mankato," he complained afterward, adding that Mankato isn't as vigilant as other communities in the fight against vice.

Soltau chided the locals for their complacency, then pledged to make a "survey" of local saloons that evening before heading back to Minneapolis.

The saloon cruising Soltau spoke under the auspices of the Minnesota Anti-Saloon League.

During the war years, material shortages precluded churches from doing repair work. As during the Depression, parishioners pitched in and did what they could. Perhaps the most ambitious war era project by church members took place in St. Peter, where men of Union Presbyterian worked by hand nights and holidays for several years to excavate a new church basement.

When it was completed, it became something of a culinary mecca. Church women became known for their roast beef dinners; men garnered praise for their pancake suppers.

An unidentified caretaker loaded coal into a furnace circa 1945 at St. John's Lutheran Church in Good Thunder.

History Glance
1940s

Hobos head out

"Hobo Jungles," shore areas of river towns that were home to homeless men, were becoming less common in smaller towns like Mankato in the mid-1900s.

In May of 1946, The Mankato Free Press interviewed one such hobo who offered these insights on the declining number of men inhabiting the "Hobo Jungle" near North Star Concrete.

According to the article, the man had just finished a breakfast of 11 slices of toast and two tin cans full of coffee when he said, "The boys have all got money this year, and they're staying close to the big city where there is plenty to do. Personally, I can't stand big cities."

"It's as easy as A, B, C," he said. He then directed the reporter's attention to a hunting jacket. "I just put my lumps, bumps and junks in there and I am off. I can't stand to let grass grow under my feet."

Snowstorm strands man and three nuns

Driver unable to get his charges through blizzard to Madison Lake convent

Emil Muellerleile, a member of All Saints Catholic Church in Madison Lake, left on a February morning in 1936 and headed to Mankato in his car to pick up three School Sisters of Notre Dame nuns and return them to their Madison Lake convent. The group left Mankato in early afternoon and headed for Madison Lake as a snowstorm gathered intensity. Snow stalled the car soon after they reached Mankato's outskirts.

Once they got going again, they pushed on for nine miles until whiteout conditions made the road virtually invisible. One of the nuns volunteered to walk ahead of the car to lead it around a bend in the road.

The storm worsened, it grew colder and Muellerleile decided enough was enough. He announced that they should venture to the nearby farmhouse of George and Theresa Daschner who, he hoped, would take them by horse team the rest of the way.

The foursome left the car and trekked to the farmhouse, where the Daschners served them a hot meal. The nuns ate in a separate room, in deference to the strict rules of Enclosure (separate dining facilities) that were then in force for women in religious orders. The storm had made conditions too foul for even horses, and the group slept at the farmhouse that night.

In the morning, Muellerleile and the hardiest of the three nuns set out on foot for Madison Lake, about two miles away. Before they left, Muellerleile gave his walking companion some practical advice:

"Now Sister, if the snow gets too deep, don't be afraid to lift your skirts, even if your ankles do show a bit."

Despite having to trudge over snowdrifts as high as the telegraph wires, in less than an hour they were at the Madison Lake convent.

Ludckes brought the 'talkies' to St. Peter

"Attend the talkies," that's what ads for the Ludcke Theater declared back around 1930.

The Ludcke Opera House was erected in 1905, with a claim of "bringing the best theatrical talent here." Movies came in 1907.

While theater and movies themselves have an interesting history, so does the Ludcke Theater.

Traveling show troupes that performed in the City Hall on the corner of Broadway and Minnesota streets in 1885 were the precursor to the theater.

Herman Ludcke was in charge of that building and his younger brother, Henry, helped him out when shows were scheduled.

When an old skating rink on Third Street was converted into a theater and dance hall in the middle 1890s, Herman Ludcke was asked to manage it because of his experience.

Fire later destroyed that theater, leaving St. Peter without a show house for six years. Eventually, local merchants convinced the brothers to build a theater of their own.

The Ludcke Opera House, on the 100 block of south Minnesota Street, enjoyed a 34-year run, taking patrons from live theater to silent movies and then on to the "talkies."

It was known as "one of the finest show houses in the state," according to news reports of the day. The Opera House also served as a hub for other activities, including high school graduations and wrestling matches.

History Glance
1940s

Housing crunch
The Mankato area, like most of America, felt the postwar housing crunch as soldiers returned home and looked for the stability of marriage and family. In October of 1947 the Mankato City Council was looking for an area to park the growing number of trailers showing up in the city, most of which housed returning military veterans and their families.

And the same month, The Free Press reported that the number of new homes and business was "unbelievable" compared to two years earlier. The assessment came from the field supervisor for R.L. Polk, which was completing work on the new city directory.

Bottle it
Fred Lutz Sr. establishes Mankato Bottling Co., which would grow into Northland Beverages, a company that eventually employed about 150 people by 1991.

Symphony orchestra began with schools

MSO formed out of local musicians, State Teachers and Gustavus colleges

One of Mankato's most prestigious arts organizations today had its origin in 1950, when local educators helped form the Mankato Symphony Orchestra.

The MSO was organized by the local musicians union, the State Teachers College, Gustavus Adolphus College and the Mankato Public Schools.

Various orchestras and musical collaborations had existed and performed throughout the area, but the MSO formed in the mid-century was the one that endured.

The MSO office today traces its roots to the efforts of May Griffin, a Boston teacher who came to Mankato in 1890 to teach at the Normal School (forerunner to Minnesota State University).

Music was thriving in the local community of just more than 10,000 residents. From 1914 on, Handel's "Messiah" had been performed almost yearly by the Mankato Orpheus Club. At the same time, a women's glee club was actively performing and a Mankato Music Club, a music appreciation group, boasted 350 members.

A symphony orchestra began playing concerts under the direction of Harold Orvis Ross.

It was Griffin who in 1922 organized 150 voices, four soloists and a full orchestra to give the largest performance yet of "Messiah." An estimated 1,700 people attended the performance, which was the largest assembly yet for a musical performance.

The MSO officially formed in 1950 and became a nonprofit corporation in 1951.

Today, as always, it consists of professionals and amateur players from around south central Minnesota. A volunteer board of directors oversees the MSO, which performs five concerts a year, each time featuring soloists often of international acclaim.

The MSO also provided opportunities for young musicians to excel through programs such as the Young Artist and Young Composer contests.

In the late 1990's, the MSO has expanded into the occasional stadium show, playing at the Mankato Civic Center with performers such as Vince Gill and the Moody Blues.

Dianne Pope has been the conductor of the MSO since 1983, and the organization planned a series of events for its 50th anniversary.

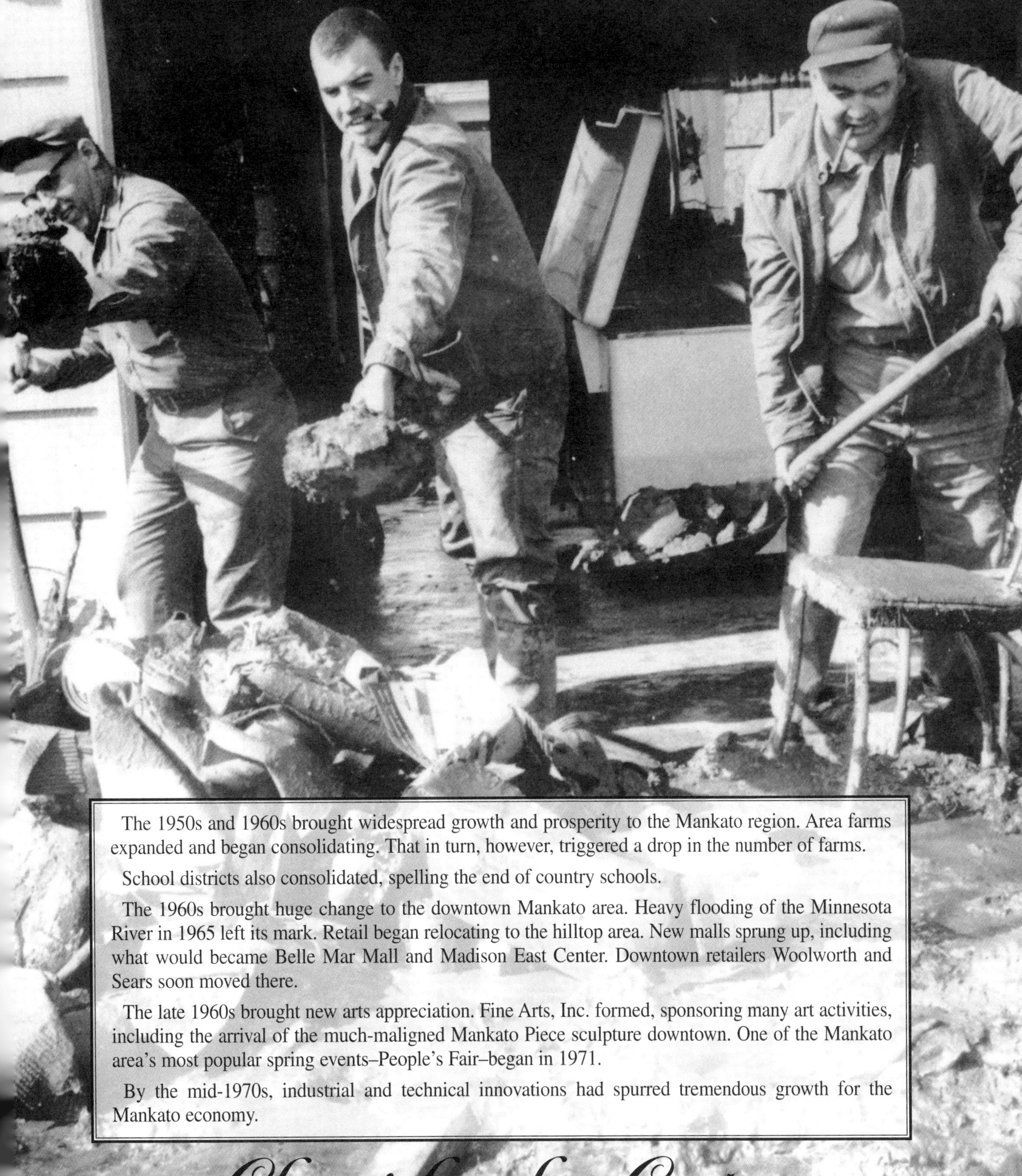

The 1950s and 1960s brought widespread growth and prosperity to the Mankato region. Area farms expanded and began consolidating. That in turn, however, triggered a drop in the number of farms.

School districts also consolidated, spelling the end of country schools.

The 1960s brought huge change to the downtown Mankato area. Heavy flooding of the Minnesota River in 1965 left its mark. Retail began relocating to the hilltop area. New malls sprung up, including what would became Belle Mar Mall and Madison East Center. Downtown retailers Woolworth and Sears soon moved there.

The late 1960s brought new arts appreciation. Fine Arts, Inc. formed, sponsoring many art activities, including the arrival of the much-maligned Mankato Piece sculpture downtown. One of the Mankato area's most popular spring events–People's Fair–began in 1971.

By the mid-1970s, industrial and technical innovations had spurred tremendous growth for the Mankato economy.

Chronicles of a Century

Part 3
1951 - 1975

Mankato economy grew with change

Industrial and technical innovations spurred growth through the '50s and '60s

St. Joseph's Hospital officials unveiled an architect's model of a planned new hospital on the hilltop, plans which came to fruition in 1953.

The third quarter of the 20th century was about industrial and technical innovation in the American economy, and Mankato was along for the ride.

"Beep, beep, beep! Something new is coming to Mankato," *The Free Press* reported in July of 1967, "and strange sounds may be heard emanating from some persons. It's all part of a new service initiated by Kost Service Inc. called a paging system."

The Free Press was willing to give Art Kost a little free publicity because this new technology was just so darned interesting. Kost had received a license a year earlier from the Federal Communications Commission, secured equipment from Motorola and signed up some customers.

"Now, after installation of the equipment, 20 individuals are able to go anyplace anywhere and be assured if someone needs them–they are only a phone call away," the newspaper reported.

Kost also offered the first primitive version of cellular phones, walkie-talkies which the company switchboard could patch phone calls to. The range was about 50 miles for the walkie-talkies and 15 to 20 miles for the pagers.

Kost said he believed the new communication system offered "a tremendous potential, but time will only tell its success."

There was innovation in materials as well.

"New Plastics Industry is formed in Mankato" was the headline from 1959, heralding the new Katolene product of National Poly Products Inc. in the former Mankato Brewing Co. building at 628 E. Rock St.

"Ten persons are employed in the around-the-clock operation of extruding polyethylene film," *The Free Press* reported.

National Poly, producing plastic film for food and product packaging, grew out of its brewery space in a decade, building a plant on Third Avenue in 1970.

And employment practices were changing too, including an early suggestion that maybe housewives might be a useful addition to the outside labor pool.

Mr. and Mrs. Charles St. John started a temporary service in August of 1968, predicting that part-time work would be a growing trend.

"It's a rather new concept for this area," Charles St. John told *The Free Press*. "And like any new concept, it takes time for it to take hold and for employers to see the applications of it to their business."

Mrs. St. John (her first name wasn't included in the story) said housewives welcome the opportunity for part-time work.

"If a woman can wake up in the morning knowing she has to get dressed to go to work, it will give her a different outlook on life," she said. "You know you get so involved with bottles and diapers that you get bogged down and forget about other things."

But despite the dramatic changes in societal and industrial trends, Mankato mainly just grew in its very methodical and traditional way. Between 1940 and 1962, 36 new industries came to Mankato, bringing the total to 106, according to a press report in February 1962. The industrial sector employed more than 3,600 people, with a payroll of nearly $11 million.

"Mankato is also a large wholesale and jobbing center with 82 businesses of this type employing 738 people with an annual payroll of $2,470,000," *The Free Press* reported. More than 140 professional people–architects, engineers, attorneys and medical professionals–served the area.

Five banks and more than 300 retail stores rounded out the local economy with estimated retail sales of $54.2 million in 1961.

And by 1973 Mankato, landlocked and a long way from anyplace foreign, had a significant stake in the global economy. A Mankato State College graduate student did a study that showed foreign markets pumped $29.6 million into the local business community in 1973.

Although the student's report didn't give specific export figures for specific companies, the local leaders in the export markets included Archer-Daniels-Midland, Midtex, Carney and Associates Inc., Electrol Equipment Inc., Johnson Reels, Kato Engineering, Katolight Corp., Minnesota Automotive, National Poly Products, Polymer Marketing Corp. and Midwest Electric Products.

The student estimated that production for export accounted for the equivalent of 175 jobs for Mankato area residents, a 50 percent increase from 1968 and representing 17 percent of all job growth in the community over the previous five years.

Retail moves out of downtown

Hilltop Florist was an early–and for years lone–hilltop business

This aerial shot of Mankato was taken during the 1950s. At that time, the city's downtown area remained its undisputed center of retail commerce.

Mankato's retail sales continued to climb in the third quarter of the century, but much of the growth occurred outside of the city's downtown.

Retailers began to follow the trail blazed by Oswald Windmiller in the 1880s. A purveyor of vegetables and flowers, he opened up his shop at the crest of Madison Avenue. The incline was called Windmiller Hill by many locals of the day. Hilltop Florist, founded by this German immigrant, was virtually the only business sitting atop the perch for many years.

In his book "A Bend in the River," Vern Lundin described how over time, a handful of other businesses made the same climb up the hill, including the Hilltop Tavern, Salfers Grove and Jolvaag's Root Beer Stand.

As car traffic along Madison Avenue built, local merchants began to recognize the opportunities for commerce east of Mankato's downtown.

On Oct. 29, 1964, Mueller's Superway opened in Eastgate Shopping Mall, the first sizeable development on Madison Avenue. The other major occupant of the center was a drug and variety store called Lewis Eastgate Drug.

In November 1964, Gamble-Skogmo opened Tempo, a 27,000-square-foot discount store in the Hilltop Shopping Center. It was the first occupant in what was to become the Belle Mar Mall.

The construction of still another new mall, the Madison Shopping Center, quickened the pace of development on the hill. The mall opened in October of 1968 and now operates as Madison East Center.

Downtown Mankato lost two of its larger retailers to the new mall: F.W. Woolworth and Sears.

"When those two pulled out, the downtown started to change," said Paul Meyer, a longtime Mankato businessman.

Woolworth opened a 45,000-square-foot store inside the new mall. It carried more than 70,000 items and featured a luncheonette that seated 82 people.

Sears became the center's largest tenant, occupying 87,000 square feet.

Madison East quickly stirred concern among downtown merchants, recalled Brett Taylor Jr., then-owner of Brett's Department Store. "We were all kind of scared of it."

Even long established downtown businesses began to migrate. In June 1969, Landkamer's, a furniture store that began downtown in 1898, relocated to a new store called the Carriage House, east of the Madison East.

The rush was on. Businesses of all sorts set up operations on the Hill.

Downtown didn't roll over, however.

The city worked to address a shortage of downtown parking for shoppers. In 1967, it built a multilevel parking ramp with 352 stalls attached to the Holiday Inn ramp. In 1970, a 449 vehicle ramp was built on Walnut Street. Another ramp with space for 1,690 vehicles was built on Pike Street (now Riverfront Drive).

There were still strong signs of life in the traditional center of Mankato.

To help generate interest in the downtown area, Brett's Department Store and First National Bank commissioned a large iron sculpture in 1968. The piece now is at the corner of Hickory Street and Riverfront Drive.

Some downtown businesses, such as Brett's, were growing, as well. In 1969, Brett's acquired the adjacent Kresge Store and quickly spread into the additional new space after remodeling.

1950s

Psychiatric changes

Breakthroughs in psychiatric care led to a decline in the population of the St. Peter State Hospital through the 1950s and beyond. The development of new tranquilizing drugs prompted marked improvements in patient behavior and allowed for discharges into the community.

The hospital's geriatric population also declined, with patients moving to many of the new nursing homes being built in Minnesota communities.

But as some of the hospital's missions were eliminated or reduced in scope, the facility faced other assignments.

In 1968, the hospital first offered treatment to the mentally retarded when 400 developmentally disabled citizens were transferred to St. Peter. In the 1970s, a treatment facility for people with alcohol and drug dependency was opened.

Madison East: 4 years in making

Hilltop shopping mall was a $2.5 million project when it opened in 1968

In October 1967, ground was broken for a Mankato shopping center that would be called Madison East. Mayor Cliff Adams is pictured here with a spadeful of dirt. The three men to the right of him are Lee Snilsberg, president of the Mankato Chamber of Commerce; Dr. R.W. Kearney, owner of the property; and R.V. Rooney, a developer from Minneapolis.

On Oct. 23, 1968, the Madison East Shopping Center officially opened, culminating four years of ideas and planning and bringing together construction, financial and retail business people from across the nation.

It is "finished," yet work continues on lesser details and negotiating with other stores to fill the remaining vacancies.

The shopping center at the intersection of Highways 14 and 22 represents a total investment of $2.5 million, and even at its opening employed several hundred persons, most from the immediate Mankato area.

The ideas, surveys, plans, work and worries all began back in 1964 when V. R. "Pat" Rooney came to Mankato from Minneapolis looking for a spot for a new Woolworth's store. Although plans for the store were later abandoned, Rooney liked what he saw in Mankato and began thinking.

Rooney, now owner and operator of several shopping centers, opened his first in Crystal, Minn., in 1955. It was a success and the business mushroomed.

"As new areas were developed, people needed places to shop," he said, "and centers were the thing."

Rooney saw that the trade area in Mankato was tremendous so machinery was put in motion. There was a market analysis, surveys of every kind and months spent in picking the right location.

"We looked everywhere and found the growth area was centered in east Mankato. Accessibility was important and the area to be served by locating there was a deciding factor."

Also, the land was available there.

Negotiations lasted about one year before Rooney finally signed a 99-year lease with Dr. R. W. Kearney for 38 acres of land on Highway 14.

Official groundbreaking was in early October 1967. Construction began on the 300,000 square-foot enclosed building and continued through the winter.

There were still many finishing touches to be added.

The parking area had to be blacktopped, something postponed due to rainy weather. Several stores had not begun and the mall was not finished. Despite all this, 12 stores were set to open.

They included Woolworth's, Sears, Madsen's, Three Sisters, Gallenkamp Shoes and Evenson's Card and Gift Shop, H and R Water Softner, Barberio Cheese Shop, Fair Snack and Singers.

Others scheduled to open included Madison East Barbers, Hi-Fashion Wig and Beauty Salon, Madison East Liquors, Sun-Kist Cleaners, Musicland and Fanny Farmer.

All told, the shopping center had room for 34 stores and extra office space.

"We have purposely left some space open so we can pick the right stores," Rooney said.

Floods disrupt business, traffic

On April 24, 1965, the Mankato Chamber of Commerce launched "Operation Bail Out," an attempt by merchants to recover after a rough winter and subsequent floods.

The Free Press described merchants' dilemma: "Shipments of merchandise have piled high because the customer traffic simply has not been able to break through the snowdrifts, the mud, the flood and more mud."

The promotional pitch went on to explain that merchants were worried that if they were unable to reduce inventories before May 1, when property tax assessments occur, they would suffer substantial losses. "Operation Bail Out" amounted to a town-wide five-day sale.

Floodwaters had disrupted traffic in Mankato, but few downtown businesses sustained any direct damage. Madsen's supermarket on the west end of town was an unfortunate exception.

The store was filled with up to four feet of water.

Consolidation ended many farms

Advances in technology and reliance of crops as income signaled a change

The 1950s and early '60s brought growth and prosperity as farmers shared in the optimism and economic strength of the time. But the early 1970s began to foreshadow severe problems soon to come to the countryside.

"There were some good times in the '50s," said Irvin Gunderson, a retired farmer from Nicollet County.

When he and his wife, Cora, bought their 160-acre farm near Norseland in 1950, it was the start of what was to be years of a strong national and local economy.

They paid $125 an acre for the farm, a relatively high price at the time. But crop and livestock prices were also strong. The Gundersons' hogs sold for about $18 a hundredweight (more than producers were getting in late 1998 during a historic slump in pork prices).

The Gundersons and other farmers were considering expansion during the good years. They built a new four bedroom house in 1957 for less than $20,000, and a new hog barn for their growing purebred Duroc hog operation.

"My first new hog barn held 180 pigs. My dad thought, 'Boy, that was way too big.' But that changed in a hurry," said Irvin, who semiretired from farming in 1962.

Gunderson said perhaps the most significant reason for the growth in crop farming in the '50s was the improvement of farm drainage.

"Probably a third of the land or more couldn't be farmed. It was too wet. They were just hay or pasture lands. Tiling is what really improved farming in this country," Gunderson said.

He said the improvement of the county drainage ditch system and the increased ease of installing farm-field drainage tile allowed much more land to be converted to crop production.

"Nicollet County has always been known for a good drainage system. I think it was a credit to the county commissioners who worked on improving the ditch system over the years."

The growing size of individual farms after World War II meant the reversal of a trend in the number of farms. After more than a half century of increases in the number of farms, the early 1950s saw the first drop in farm numbers. From 1949 to 1954 Blue Earth and Nicollet counties lost about 2 percent of their farms.

In 1954, more than 96 percent of the land in Blue Earth County was farmland, according to a report by the Extension Service. The average farm size was 164 acres.

An acre of farm land in the Mankato area was selling for $198.

The average cash receipts for a 1954 farm locally totalled $8,576. About half that income was from crops, 21 percent from hogs, 11 percent from beef and the remainder from dairy and other livestock.

Indeed, crops were increasingly the main source of income for most farmers in the 1950s, '60s and early '70s. Before World War II, less than 40 percent of local farm income was from crops, with most farm income from livestock.

The beginning of growth and consolidation in farming had an impact on another longtime hallmark of rural Minnesota–the creamery.

Through the '30s and '40s there were a dozen or more creameries in each of the area counties. But a combination of events spelled the death of most of them by the early 1970s.

Many blamed the closure of creameries on the Milkhouse Law, which banned putting milk into the old-fashioned milk cans. Others say the creameries closed because of farmers' increased reliance on crop production and the consolidation and growth of large milk cooperatives.

By the mid '60s there were only a handful of creameries still operating and a decade later, the number of area creameries could be counted on one hand.

While tractors and pull behind machinery were in full use by the 1950s, there were significant advances in harvesting equipment.

Combines became self-propelled in the 1950s and the first picker-sheller combine came on the market in 1957.

In the late 1960s, homeowners and farmers were singing the praises of the new Cub Cadet tractors, which came with optional equipment such as snow blower, mower and a yard fertilizer.

History Glance
1950s

Tuning in

One of the most popular products to burst onto the retail scene during the 1950s was the television.

Paul Meyer, former owner of Meyer & Sons Appliance, said his shop was the first in Mankato to carry color televisions. Although they sold for about $500 to $600 - a sum that Meyer said was "a lot of money at that time"–they still sold quickly.

Residents of the Minnesota River Valley had to work for decent reception. Until 1960, when KEYC established a local TV station in North Mankato, Meyer said residents often had to install antennas that were 30 to 40 feet high to get any channels.

50 bushels an acre

By 1950 commercial fertilizer use had increased average corn yields to 50 bushels per acre.

Farmers worked 12 hours to produce 100 bushels of corn using a tractor, three-bottom plow, disk, harrow, four-row planter and two-row picker.

Area farmer attracted notoriety

Outspoken advocate of alfalfa production started world plowing contest

Bert Hanson built this 60-by-208-foot confined slatted-floor cattle feeding barn and four Harvestore silos on the Bill Noy Jr. farm near Vernon Center in 1970. The barn, which held 600 cattle, was paid for by the first 1,200 cattle to be fed in it. The farm was the site of the 1972 world plowing contest, which drew hundreds of thousands of visitors.

One of the most colorful, successful farmers and farm advocates in the area was Bert Hanson, a farmer who championed the production of alfalfa, traveled the world and spoke to thousands of farm groups across the country.

Hanson and his wife, Irene, began farming on his parents' Nicollet County farm in the 1920s and later bought another farm in the Vernon Center area in Blue Earth County. He was born in 1901, retired in 1973 and died in 1989.

Hanson was a strong-willed man who often shocked his neighbors and audiences with his strong opinions, according to the book "Beyond the Furrow," by Hiram Drache of Concordia College. But Hanson also had a knack for gaining respect for his success and opinions, even by those who were unsettled by his sometimes harsh manner, according to Drache.

Perhaps Hanson's lifetime achievement was his role in bringing worldwide attention to the area in 1972 when he helped organize the World Plowing Contest in Vernon Center.

The contest was held on 1,400 acres of land owned by 14 farmers, with Hanson donating his entire farm for use in the event. Thirty-six seed corn companies planted 600 acres of corn and 130 acres of soybeans. The remainder of the land was dedicated to demonstrations, competitive events and parking. More than 500,000 people attended the seven-day event.

Hanson first gained local and national notoriety in 1929 for purchasing the first John Deere corn planter with fertilizer boxes in Minnesota. Hanson secured three tons of fertilizer on the first carload of commercial fertilizer ever shipped to Mankato.

But Hanson was best known in the national agricultural community for alfalfa. While most farmers were reducing the amount of alfalfa they were growing in favor of corn and soybeans, Hanson maintained his alfalfa fields and dramatically increased production.

From 1951 to 1973, when he retired, he produced an amazing 1,200 to 1,400 pounds of beef per acre each year. He consistently produced more than twice the average amount of alfalfa per acre than other farmers in the county.

Word of Hanson's success with alfalfa production and beef cattle spread across the nation and he began speaking to farm groups in virtually every state and parts of Canada.

He gave some 900 talks as a sponsor for the A.O. Smith company, which made Harvestore silos. Indeed, the Harvestore became a central success in Hanson's farm and business operations.

The glass-lined steel silage, haylage and grain storage units had an air system that controlled the oxygen that came in contact with the stored feed. The units cut down on harvesting time and allowed for automated feeding of Hanson's cattle.

Hanson praised the Harvestores and said haylage or silage never spoiled in his silos. But the Harvestore came under assault in the 1980s as farmers across the nation joined in class action lawsuits claiming the Harvestores had design flaws that caused millions of dollars in losses. Many of the lawsuits were settled or ruled in favor of the farmers, leading to the end of the once-mighty Harvestore.

Bert Hanson, shown in a 1962 photo, was an outspoken farm advocate from Vernon Center.

Peas were a cash crop

Corn, small grain and soybeans were the chief local cash crops in the 1950s and '60s, but vegetable farming was also significant.

Irvin Gunderson, who farmed near Norseland, remembered many farmers who raised peas for the Green Giant Co. in Le Sueur.

In the 1940s and into the early 1950s many farmers cut the pea vines in the field with horse-pulled mowers or tractor-operated mowers.

The pea vines were then pitched by hand onto a wagon and hauled to a central neighborhood location, where a pea viner machine cracked the peas out of the shell and deposited the chopped up vines in a pile for use as silage.

"The peas would go into boxes, and when there was a truck full, they'd take them to Le Sueur," Gunderson said.

Time phased out country school

Consolidation of rural and small-town school districts led to change

In the late 1960s, Rosetta Hislop was a living relic.

She taught at a tiny white school on a hill six miles outside of Amboy. Willow Creek, as it was called, had an enrollment of six students. Music classes consisted of time spent around the piano, and physical education consisted of games played in the yard. Hislop rented living quarters with a nearby family during the school year.

But that era was over, and Hislop and her school were anomalies. For years, tiny schools were built at a machine-gun pace. By the 1950s, bigger was better.

M.L. Wolverton, Mankato East High School's first principal, showed off the new commons area before furniture was hauled into the building. The school opened in 1973.

Six Blue Earth County school districts faced a consolidation mandate in the late 1960s: Eagle Lake, Judson, Madison Lake, Sugar Grove, Vernon Center and Willow Creek. These districts didn't have high schools, so they were forced to merge with a high school district. Willow Creek and Sugar Grove were the last remaining country schools.

Bigger schools meant more course offerings, a broader tax base and more state funding. In some cases, it meant improved quality. A Rapidan home economics teacher in 1969, for example, also taught algebra and science in her school. Bigger schools had teachers who specialized in their areas of instruction.

Larger districts were banding together as well. Mankato and North Mankato schools consolidated in 1957. With the increasing number of neighboring students coming to Mankato, it was clear the new Mankato High School wouldn't be large enough.

School officials began to study in the issue in 1963, but a citizen advisory group wasn't formed until 1970. The district put together an $11.5 million bond issue that included a new $9 million high school on the hill and other facilities projects. The measure passed in 1970 in a record voter turnout.

Mankato East High School opened in 1973 and the community was excited. Open house organizers figured they served cookies to more than 6,000 people touring the school.

Older buildings, however, were seeing their last days. St. Peter School officials began pointing out the age of Central Elementary, a building that had sentimental value to many town residents. (It had been a high school as well.)

Parents and former graduates had temporary success in keeping the turn-of-the-century building open. Ultimately, it was closed as a school and rented out for community uses until the 1998 tornado left it in ruins.

Meanwhile, postsecondary institutions also were growing.

The Mankato Area Vocational-Technical Institute moved to upper North Mankato from its makeshift accommodations in Mankato.

Mankato State's downtown campus was abandoned, and the new hilltop campus was developed and expanded.

Consolidation trend quickens

The death of the country school and wave of school consolidations began in the early-to-middle part of the century, but its pace jumped considerably in the 1950s and 1960s.

In 1938, Blue Earth County alone had 91 school districts with their own schools. Another 21 districts sent their students elsewhere. Nicollet County had 60 school districts in the early part of the century.

Rural residents didn't want their children to walk too far, so one-room schools popped up every couple of miles. Early state law said a district needed at least five families to form. If there were 10 or more families, the district could divide into two districts.

The districts slowly began combining as state aid became tied to enrollment: More students meant more money. One-room country schools had trouble competing with impressive new town schools that had electricity, sports programs and hot lunch.

On Feb. 19, 1953, the Mapleton School Board accepted no less than 20 rural school districts in a consolidation move after both the city and rural residents approved the move in a vote.

But some rural areas fought consolidation. Eagle Lake had intense debates in the 1950s about abandoning its 75-year-old school–which already had survived a fire–and joining with Mankato. On Dec. 9, 1958, residents voted 3 to 1 against the Mankato consolidation, even though there were concerns the state wouldn't approve a new school because of the small population base.

The state finally pushed a consolidation mandate in the 1960s: Districts without high schools should join a high school district by 1971. By 1964, Eagle Lake had its new elementary school, but its secondary students went either to Mankato or St. Clair. In 1969, Eagle Lake consolidated with Mankato but kept its building.

The consolidation of rural districts continues to this day.

Teacher experienced all the changes over decades

Education has shifted as society and students have changed, Stoufer says

Roger Stoufer

If Hollywood made a movie called "Mr. Stoufer's Opus," the themes from three decades of his life in education would play out something like this:

The mythical innocence of the '50s is no myth. Roger Stoufer graduates with a class of 22 students from Echo in the late '50s. He doesn't drink because kids don't do much of that, they fear their parents. Neighbors keep a watchful eye on all the kids and report any misdeeds. Stoufer doesn't learn the meaning of "gay lifestyle" until he turns 20.

Fast forward to the '60s.

Now a teacher in Stewart, Stoufer, like other married male teachers, earns more than his female counterparts because he is, after all, the head of a household. Girls wear skirts to class; boys remember to take off their hats at the door–or else. The president is shot, and a school banquet turns into an impromptu memorial with strong religious overtones. As the years pass, boys' hair gets longer, and people start talking about a growing military conflict in Vietnam.

On to the '70s.

A junior high teacher in Mankato since 1965, Stoufer and his colleagues watch social unrest slowly unfold in their classrooms. Kids get bolder: they puff cigarettes in front of his classroom window; some are believed to be smoking pot. Stoufer finds himself debating the merits of the war with a young student teacher who wants time off work to protest (Stoufer's support wanes toward the end). Special education students are segregated in different rooms; but girls, freed from their dresses, begin to get active in sports.

This section ends in the '70s, but Stoufer also survived the '80s and '90s before retiring and finding himself elected to the board that will lead Mankato Area Public Schools into the new millennium.

Looking back over his career, Stoufer said it's no cliché: "Things were simpler, like the movies portrayed it. The big problems in general were focused on ourselves. We weren't very worldly, and our kids weren't very worldly."

Stoufer, however, didn't see the past in black and white. Social changes had positive and negative ramifications. On one hand, girls' freedom meant more academic opportunities and success in sports. But with that freedom, for example, came sexual experimentation that resulted in more teen pregnancies.

Yet he saw black-and-white views come and go: when he was a young student, he was "de-pantsed" on the bus. Then, it was a funny joke, a ritual of youth.

"If that behavior happened today, you'd be sued."

Behavior shifts are fine, but he worried about it going too far.

"I don't want to see schools lose all the playfulness. Kids have to learn, but at the same time, there has to be a little bit of joy in the classroom."

Although the '50s and '60s were a more innocent time, Stoufer said kids weren't angels. They skipped school and played pranks, but the trouble they caused wasn't serious. The increasing acceptance of drugs and alcohol and the way chemical use has trickled into younger and younger ages has changed the meaning of trouble.

"When kids get hooked into chemical use, they get mean. We weren't mean. We were playful."

Stoufer earned his teaching degree from Mankato State University, and he taught both history and English. Early in his career in Mankato, he taught junior high students at Lincoln School and then high school at West. During his last few years, he was principal at the Alternative High School.

The biggest changes in schools, he said, was their evolution from mostly academics to the mammoth responsibilities they have today: after-school activity planners, drug counselors, breakfast providers, social workers and latch-key programmers.

The best change, he said, was the surge in girls' sports. He remembered when he and another teacher brought girls onto the school's gymnastic team before they were supposed to.

Academically, Stoufer believed the most significant improvement was the shift away from a one-size-fits-all teaching approach. The way educators teach reading has improved, for instance, because there is a recognition that different kids learn to read differently.

"That's exciting," he said. "We used to put students in the same box and expect them all to learn in the same way."

1950s

Fatal train collision

A train engineer was killed and seven passengers injured in 1951 when two locomotives collided near Mankato.

A passenger train traveling 40 mph and a freight train traveling 35 mph collided after a signal operator in Lake Crystal failed to stop the passenger train when it came through his town.

About 25 sheep also were killed.

Flooded out

Bill and Betty Carlson ran their printing company (later known as Carlson Craft and, ultimately, part of the conglomerate Taylor Corp.) from their home until their home was destroyed by floods in 1951.

After two temporary locations, the company with its 20 employees, moved to rental space at 511 South Front St. in Mankato in 1953.

War spawned technical schools

South Central Technical College has its roots in this small garage, which was the site of the first training program. Pictured here are the first class members of what was called the Mankato Area Technical College.

The large vocational college campus in North Mankato was built in 1968, but it has its roots in events that occurred two decades earlier.

World War II veterans returned home, and lawmakers wanted them to have good jobs. They pumped money into tuition programs that helped vets pay for their education, and the government set up new training institutions.

Meanwhile, rural leaders concluded they had to compete with big cities for industry to keep small-town economies strong.

Area technical schools were founded on the premise that outstate Minnesota needed a trained labor force to attract and maintain industry. Federal lawmakers were interested in this trend as well: the Soviet Union's launch of Sputnik in 1957 prompted concerns that the U.S. would fall behind in technology. Money was pumped into technical programs.

South Central Technical College, as it is now called, began as the Mankato Area Vocational-Technical Institute in 1947 with 94 students and eight teachers. Before that, workers typically were trained at plants in the area.

Private ventures attempted to do the same training. The Mankato Commercial College was operated from 1891 to 1944, when it was bought by another family. It closed in 1980, unable to compete with the state schools.

The state program grew tremendously and a second building opened in Mankato in 1949, with an addition 10 years later. Finally, a third permanent building was constructed in upper North Mankato. A $6 million expansion occurred in the late 1980s.

Since then, the state's technical colleges have merged with its universities.

Transportation takes to the air

Bus service declines while passenger trains fade away in the 1960s

Downtown streets in Mankato were lined with dealerships that sold dozens of different kinds of vehicles in the 1950s. Among them was this Indian motorcycle, parked on the 200 block of South Second Street in 1953.

While passenger train service dwindled and finally died, air travel became increasingly common and bus ridership went from record highs to desperate lows.

Five railroads served Mankato in the 1950s: Chicago and North Western, Chicago Great Western, Chicago-Milwaukee-St. Paul and Pacific, Chicago-Minneapolis-St. Paul and Omaha, and Milwaukee Road. Only two offered passenger routes. By 1963, however, the last passenger train rolled through Mankato.

A stickier transportation issue in the 1960s and 1970s involved bus service to Mankato and North Mankato.

In 1973, Mankato City Lines Inc., the company that had provided bus service to both cities since 1936, threatened to stop running buses unless it got financial help from cities to buffer it from the financial strain of low ridership.

Although the company grew from one bus in 1936 to 22 buses in 1968–and ridership crept toward a half million riders annually–it couldn't survive a declining customer base that hit in the late 1960s. The problem was solved when the cities agreed to buy the operation and commence municipal ownership of the bus line.

Several years later, the future of buses was threatened when both councils wrestled with the idea of scrapping bus service in favor of some other form of mass transit. Experts came in to brief the council on different methods of mass transit, including light rail, bus and mini bus. Both councils eventually opted for traditional bus service and a few mini buses.

Air travel became increasingly common each decade. By the 1950s, several airlines were providing passenger flights out of Mankato daily from the hilltop airport, near today's university campus. The major carrier in the early days of passenger flight was Western Airlines, at the time the nation's oldest airline. Western left the airport in the 1960s.

Flight reached new heights in the 1960s with the dawning of the jet age. In 1967, jets prompted the need for a new municipal airport with longer runways. After several contentious council meetings and minor opposition from area farmers, the City Council approved building a new airport. It chose a site about six miles north of the city in Lime Township, where it sits today.

The new facility opened in 1970 and cost about $3 million. At the time, the airport's major tenant was North Central Airline, then the nation's largest air carrier.

In 1970, a helicopter landed on the roof of the Second Street ramp. It was designed to act as an alternative transportation mode to airplanes or cars for people traveling to the Twin Cities. Helicopter flights cost about $18 to Minneapolis.

Automobiles continued to dominate, as did the need for roadways to support them. Tens of millions of dollars were being spent annually to add roads or improve existing ones.

Passenger trains stopped in 1963

Train travel slumped so badly in the 1960s that, by the middle of the decade, the final passenger trains had left Mankato and St. Peter.

Five railroads served Mankato in the 1950s: Chicago and North Western, Chicago Great Western, Chicago-Milwaukee-St. Paul and Pacific, Chicago-Minneapolis-St. Paul and Omaha, and Milwaukee Road.

The Milwaukee Road rail line hauled its last Mankato passengers in 1951. In 1963, the Chicago and North Western Rail Line saw its final passengers.

Those were the last passenger trains to roll through Mankato.

The final voyage was on Chicago and North Western's "Famous 400," a train that excited riders in the 1930s with its air conditioning and luxury ride.

The 400 took just over six hours to travel from Mankato to Chicago. Its name came from the number of minutes the trip took.

Declining numbers forced trains to shift from hauling passengers to freight.

In 1951 the volume of freight handled in Mankato was 45 percent inbound and 55 percent outbound.

But in 1960, the prominence of trains was on the decrease. In that year, according to the St. Peter Herald, railroads were abandoning about 200 miles of rail lines every year.

People's Fair was small at the start

The debut of the annual festival drew about 100 people to ball field

People's Fair in 1972 was in its infancy, eventually becoming an annual attraction drawing thousands to a weekend's worth of music in Sibley Park.

The first People's Fair was far from the massive fest of music, bodies and beer that in recent years has drawn more than 10,000.

The first People's Fair in June 1971 drew about 100 to the lawn of the Mankato State College ball field on lower campus, now a parking lot for Old Main Village.

Three groups handed out fliers while a local band played acid rock.

It lasted from 3 p.m. to midnight, with the donations raised going to a walk-in crisis center called Eclipse, which helped people facing VD and drug problems.

The following year, the festival moved to Sibley Park, featuring local bands including City Mouse and the Dust Bowl Blues Band.

In just five years, however, the estimated number of people who attended was 12,000.

In 1978, organizers turned it into a two-day affair, with the second day devoted to bluegrass music.

Musical acts appearing at People's Fair include Little Feat, The Wailers, Michael Johnson and dozens of local acts.

Today, the festival still benefits Eclipse, as well as the Volunteer Center and other local charities.

History Glance
1960s

KEYC plays ball

KEYC television station's first broadcast was the 1960 World Series.

The station was the first building in Minnesota constructed just to house a television studio, according to the Nicollet County Historical Society. Others were housed in old office buildings.

The station's first newscast was at 10 p.m. Oct. 16, 1960, with the 6 p.m. newscast starting the following day.

Hardware store closes

In 1966, the A.A. Zimmerman Hardware Store, 215 N. Front St., was closed and the building auctioned.

The Mankato family business had survived for about 90 years.

Mankato Piece part of arts in town

Fine Arts Inc. fostered appreciation of arts for more than a decade

Sculptor Dale Eldred's 'Mankato Piece' is a 72-ton iron structure constructed in 1968. It has remained a conversation piece for more than 30 years.

The middle and late 1960s saw an acceleration of fine art appreciation and activities in Mankato, fostered and inspired largely by a group called Fine Arts Inc.

Art in the Park was one of Fine Arts Inc.'s activities, along with community theater, a film series, a community chorus, art classes and creative writing. Family memberships into the group cost $7.50.

Fine Arts Inc., not funded publicly, sustained itself on individual and corporate memberships.

The organization was instrumental in arranging creation of the most controversial art development in the community, the steel girder sculpture dubbed The Mankato Piece.

The Mankato Piece was a modern sculpture by Minneapolis native Dale Eldred. The criss-crossed steel beams were originally at a confining location on Hickory Street between Front and Second streets.

Eldred's work was, in his own words, "severe and graphic," which also matched much of the criticism the piece generated. In 1981, the work was moved behind the Mankato Mall parking ramp along Riverfront Drive.

It was moved because its site was being taken over by the Heco office-residential complex. The decision on where it should be relocated prompted two public meetings.

Although it was suggested that Mankato State University would be a good home, the City Council decided the sculpture should remain downtown for greater visibility, and the site chosen at Riverfront and Hickory would provide better protection against vandalism.

To this day, the work is an ongoing topic of debate, ranging from its artistic merit to the cost of its upkeep.

When it was dismantled for the 1981 move, it sat in pieces near the Holiday Inn parking ramp throughout an entire winter. Eventually it was reconstructed the next May for $34,425, the cost of which was split by the city and the developers of the Heco building.

In 1995, the Piece became the focal point of another argument over the cost of paint. Council members debated whether or not the Piece needed to be painted. The cost came in at $25,840. Without paint, the Piece would rust and crumble.

By contrast, it was also suggested that rusting and crumbling was–perhaps–in line with what the sculptor had in mind as a statement on progress.

The decision was made to paint it.

It's likely a situation Eldred would have appreciated. The artist was best known for his massive metal and wood pieces and large works that interacted with sunlight.

Since the Mankato Piece, Eldred's works were installed in cities around the world, and in 1983 he installed reflective and light-bending panels around the Minneapolis Institute of Arts.

In 1993, Eldred died at age 59 in an accident at his art studio in Kansas City. He had been moving pieces from one floor to another to prevent them being damaged by rising flood waters and stepped through an opening on the second floor and fell 20 feet.

Robert Finkler, chairman of Mankato State University's art department, said at the time: "Mankato is really quite fortunate to have that piece. It's unfortunate that it's been in some of the situations it's been in. But it is remarkable that Mankato was able to have such a thing."

Recognition of the piece came early. In January 1969, the Mankato Fine Arts Inc. was one of 13 Minnesota arts organizations to receive a special state award for contributing to the artistic climate of the state, particularly for arranging the Mankato Piece sculpture.

Louis Zell, chairman of the State Arts Council, cited the Fine Arts organization "for the initiative taken in developing and following through with the plans for the Dale Eldred sculpture in downtown Mankato."

Also honored among the 13 was Sir Tyrone Guthrie, founder of the Guthrie Theater in Minneapolis.

The Mankato Piece was featured prominently in a 1978 book by Ralph T. Coe titled "Dale Eldred: Sculpture Into Environment."

On March 14, 1969, the Fine Arts Inc. opened a gallery at Front and Cherry streets, calling it Gallery 500. It was the organization's first permanent exhibition area, and in March 1972, one of its biggest shows featured original works by artists including Andy Warhol and Jasper Johns. The exhibit ran for a month, on loan from Dayton's.

The Gallery moved to 112 Grove St. in 1973, in the process losing a gallery but gaining various rooms for art education. In 1975, because of a depressed economy, declining involvement and what columnist Ken Berg called "a valleying of art consciousness," the Fine Arts Inc.–which for 12 years had rallied the community around the arts and vice versa–ended.

Art in the Park festival fills Mankato with a wide variety and quality of art

Art in the Park was one of the events launched by the homegrown organization Fine Arts Inc.

The group's first major activity was a fine arts festival, which began in 1963.

The idea gained momentum through the years and in October 1966, Sibley Park was host to a large outdoor art exhibit, featuring a Minneapolis judge, cash prizes donated by Honeymead and music by a woodwind quintet.

The next year, art remained a strong community presence, demonstrated by the Fine Arts Festival's influence beyond its Hickory Street location.

Works of art for the festival were displayed at *The Free Press*, City Hall, banks and Mankato State College.

The event also showcased the area's talents in painting, photography, music and sculpture.

A bandshell featured the Mankato High School Chorus, a dancing ensemble, Good Counsel Academy Choir and the Mankato Youth Symphony.

In 1968, the turnout for Art in the Park at Sibley drew hundreds, as well as an enthusiastic response from *Free Press* critic Roy Close (later was a theater critic for the *St. Paul Pioneer Press*).

"Art in the Park provides as much contrast in media, styles and ability in art as Mankato can offer," Close wrote, marveling at both the high quality and low quality of the art displayed.

"It's well worth the drive and a battle for a parking space."

Joint services help save on fuel costs

Three churches find other benefits in 1974 ecumenical experiment

The national fuel shortage fostered ecumenism in the winter of 1974.

Three Mankato churches, First Baptist, First Congregational and Centenary United Methodist, decided to cut fuel costs by holding joint worship services.

It was decided that the services would be held at the Methodist church during January and February.

"It was initiated by our people as a Christian effort to become involved with the problems of our country," Methodist Pastor William Kvale said at the time.

"It's not just an ecumenical exercise or a scramble to avoid fuel-shortage problems. It's a Christian statement."

So while the Methodist church served as the central gathering place, the other churches shut down, drained their water pipes to prevent freezing and heated only office spaces.

Ministers rotated conducting services, and church secretaries shared the duty of preparing the Sunday bulletins. Meanwhile, the ministers discovered they now had greater opportunity to minister.

"I've had a lot more time for calls on our members when another pastor was leading the service," Kvale said.

Parishioners said they liked the joint services just fine.

"Oh, yes, I feel quite comfortable," said Congregationalist Ethel Selix.

"Of course, I know some people here. But we've met new ones, too, haven't we?" she said to companion Myrtle Steiner.

History Glance
1970s

Here's another example that it wasn't so long ago that everything automatic was new and exciting. The Free Press did a photo spread on Feb. 15, 1973, about the new automatic parking gate at Landkamer's Funeral Home and Landkamer's Furniture Store.

In an attempt to control access to the crowded parking lot, Landkamer's introduced the first coin-operated gate to the Mankato area. Readers were told how they could pull up to the gate, grab a ticket from the machine to get the gate to lift and then exit after inserting a free token obtained from Landkamer's.

A few people were confused and uncertain of the correct procedure, but none tried to force the gates, a Landkamer's official said.

Ramy Seed Co.

Ramy Seed Co., known to most farmers as a firm that produces non-corn seed, announced it has 10 varieties of seed corn. The new products were developed after the company's purchase of Embro Seed Co. of St. Louis, Missouri three years earlier and involved tests done at its research farm near Lake Crystal.

Speaking of religious changes

Latin gives way to English in Catholic masses; German services fade at Nicollet Lutheran church

A pulpit's-eye view of St. John's Lutheran Church of Vernon Center in the late 1960s took in a packed house at Sunday services.

This era marked what might be described as a period of modernism in local churches.

The influences of German and Scandinavian church founders continued to lessen as churches became more Americanized in their worship services.

At Trinity Evangelical Lutheran in Nicollet, German-language services that had been held every Sunday since the 19th century were cut back to two Sundays a month. In 1965, they were cut back further, to six a year.

Catholic churches underwent even more profound transformations in the mid-1960s following the Second Vatican Council, popularly known as Vatican II.

During that period, Masses celebrated in English in the United States (and in native tongues in the rest of the Western world) displaced the uniform Latin Mass that had been used for centuries. This permitted more lay participation in the Mass. Lectors and commentators read parts of the Mass, and congregation singing was inaugurated.

Also, the priest now faced the congregation while offering Mass from a free-standing altar that was nearer to parishioners than the former altars.

The middle part of the century also saw churches expand their social roles in members' lives. In 1961, the Men's Club dartball team from Immanuel Lutheran of Courtland won the state tournament.

Tempering these upswings were periodic hardships that randomly befell congregations. In April 1951, low-lying churches weren't spared the ravages of massive flooding along the Minnesota River.

One church, St. Paul's Evangelical Lutheran in North Mankato, saw its basement flooded to a depth of 6½ feet. No services were held there until mid-May.

The early '60s marked two other disasters. On Nov. 12, 1960, a gas explosion leveled the new Evangelical Covenant Church in North Mankato and two years later a lightning fire destroyed First Lutheran in St. Peter. Its 1,400 parishioners worshipped at Gustavus Adolphus College in St. Peter until a new $523,000 church was completed in 1964.

The era also saw the founding of congregations.

In the early '50s, growth in the West Mankato area prompted the founding of St. Joseph the Worker Catholic Church.

Also during that period, eight Baptist men anxious to see their children regularly attend Sunday School formed the underpinnings of Grace Baptist in North Mankato.

Concrete for the chapel floor was poured Feb. 2, 1953. It was, church historians noted, the only night that winter that the temperature didn't dip below freezing.

With the help of the Rev. John Michel, now pastor of Grace Baptist but then a student at Mankato State College, the church and its fledgling Youth Ministry prospered.

In the early 1960s, Grace Baptist began airing a weekly Sunday religious telecast on KEYC-TV in North Mankato. The broadcast still airs and still has Michel as its host.

Development of the Mankato hilltop area also spurred church growth. In September 1972, Hosanna Lutheran held its first organizational meeting in Pastor Bruce Zagel's living room. Two years later, Hosanna held its first service in its new building.

Meanwhile, modernization of religious services continued to evolve, largely as a means of attracting young worshippers.

At St. John's Episcopal in Mankato in the mid-1960s, some traditionalists looked askance at services that now incorporated folk music. But Pastor Timothy Hallett stood his ground.

"We make no apologies for being ecumenical and contemporary in our program," he said.

1970s

Main Street Bridge

On Jan. 4, 1971, a structural weakness changed the Main Street Bridge from a three- to a two-lane thoroughfare.

The bridge, built in 1917, had operated for two years as a three-lane road, with two opposing lanes and a center turning lane.

But a Highway Department investigation revealed the bridge was failing about four feet from the curb, a weakness that, if it worsened, could have prohibited large vehicles from crossing the river.

The department repaired the bridge the following summer. The bridge eventually was replaced in 1986.

Cotter and Co.

Mankato celebrates landing a new warehouse after wooing Cotter and Co., the world's largest hardware wholesaler, to the city with tax-increment financing.

A $3.5 million 300,000-square-foot distribution center would be constructed by 1976 on Third Avenue near the soon-to-be built Highway 14 bypass.

Big business began small

Engineering company Bolton & Menk Inc. started running on empty

Martin Menk, a founder of Bolton & Menk engineering firm, and his partner John Bolton filled a niche providing consulting engineering services for cities and municipalities that has continued over the years.

John Bolton and Martin Menk started their engineering business with empty pockets.

They got their equipment on credit from a supplier Bolton knew from his days as a professor at Gustavus Adolphus College, who told them they could pay when they made money.

Their first office was in a 12-foot by 20-foot building–a size that could easily be sold off as a garage if the business didn't work out. It didn't have a restroom, so they used the nearby filling station.

Fifty years later, their firm, Bolton & Menk Inc., had more than 130 employees with offices in Mankato, Fairmont, Sleepy Eye, Burnsville and Willmar, as well as Ames, Iowa, and Liberty, Mo.

"I'm just amazed," said Menk. "I didn't think that would ever happen."

A St. Peter native, Menk returned to his hometown after serving in the Navy during World War II. As a student, he met Bolton, a former Penn State University professor, at Gustavus.

Menk considered him both mentor and friend.

Menk later graduated from Washington State University. At the time, Gustavus was phasing out its pre-engineering program in favor of a more liberal arts curriculum. The program was put in place to train engineers during the war.

The two men decided to go into business together in 1949, finding a niche providing consulting engineering services for cities and other municipalities, a market the firm still captures today.

"We wondered what the little towns around southern Minnesota did for engineering, towns that didn't have enough work for a full-time engineer," Menk said.

Vernon Center, Lake Crystal, Madelia, Lewisville, Truman and St. James were some of the firm's early customers. The engineers designed all the Vernon Center streets in about 1950.

Housing developments boomed after the war, keeping Bolton and Menk busy surveying lots and planning subdivisions.

Together, they worked on sewer systems, streets, curbs, gutters and wastewater treatment centers–some of the often-overlooked niceties of city living.

"You're helping build the physical plan of the community," Menk said. "The people make up the community and the people do the rest."

Menk said he particularly enjoyed the problem-solving end of the business, watching the communities grow and getting to know city council members and other residents.

Bolton & Menk picked up more business (and more employees) each year, partly because of its philosophy of doing quality work, satisfying the customer and building relationships.

Menk himself served as city engineer for St. Peter for some 30 years, prompting city officials to name a street, Menk Drive, after him in honor of his years of service. He also served as North Mankato engineer for some 20 years.

Bolton retired from the firm in 1965 to pursue other interests. He died in 1990. Menk retired in 1992.

Menk said it wasn't uncommon for veterans to come back from the war and start their own businesses or take over others.

"It was pretty well organized," he said. "There was the need for services. There were the people to do it. Whether they did it because they wanted to forget the war, I don't know. It's possible."

While small businesses were all the rage back in the '50s, Menk said the '60s were marked with consolidation with larger businesses.

For example, there were several one-man engineering firms throughout southern Minnesota, including Le Center, Blue Earth, Fairmont, Gaylord, Owatonna and Sleepy Eye early on.

Firms such as Bolton & Menk bought out others when the engineers were ready to retire or try something new. The firm took over an office in Blue Earth, as well as one in Willmar in the '60s.

In 1966, Bolton & Menk moved its St. Peter office to Mankato for a more centralized location to its growing customer base.

Looking back, Menk said he and Bolton were lucky, even though they put in long hours of hard work. A dream wouldn't be enough to get a business going today.

"We'll have entrepreneurs forever, but I think it gets more difficult to do. It would be hard for someone to start a business again like we started ours, but it could be done."

Martin Menk recalled the entrepreneurship that followed World War II. That's when Menk of St. Peter, started his engineering firm, Bolton & Menk, with John Bolton. Now in Mankato, the business marked its 50th anniversary in 1999.

Businesses started in basements

Carlson Craft, Sween Corp. and Hermel all worked way upstairs

It all started in the basement. That was the case for William Carlson, founder of Carlson Craft, and for Maurice "Al" Sween, founder of Sween Corp.

Both began their multi-million dollar businesses in the cellars of their houses, eventually bringing them to North Mankato.

Sween developed a non-aerosol deodorant called Hex-On and then Sween Cream, a hand and body lotion, at his home in 1964. Two salesmen friends sold the products to hospitals and nursing homes.

Sween Corp. operated out of locations in Rapidan, Lake Crystal and Mankato before settling on Commerce Drive in 1989, where it became a $20 million-plus multi-national business. The company was acquired by Coloplast A/S of Denmark in 1995.

Another local business, the Hermel Candy and Tobacco Co., was also in full swing after starting in Adolph Hermel's St. Peter home in 1935.

The business was on Minnesota Avenue where the AmericInn Motel is today. A Quonset hut in the backyard also housed some operations.

Hermel's sons, Cliff and Howard, later took over the business, now run by Howard's son, David.

The company moved to rural Mankato in 1968.

Development and diversification brought boom times for the Mankato area overall in this period, but the 1980's farm crisis left its mark on the region.

In Mankato, nonagricultural businesses blunted the impact of the farm crisis. New computer and service-oriented businesses developed. Local theater and live music blossomed.

The Mankato Mall opened downtown in 1978, with initial success followed by tough times that prompted the city to take ownership. Perhaps the biggest development came in 1991, when River Hills Mall opened–the largest retail shopping center between Sioux Falls, S.D., and Rochester. That triggered phenomenal retail growth on the city's eastern edge that continued through 1999, but also took a bite out of business for Madison East Center and the Mankato Mall.

The opening of the Civic Center in 1995 helped boost Mankato's downtown activity. And North Mankato saw unprecedented growth, both residential and commercial, in its hilltop area.

The 1990s also brought large-scale natural disaster to the region: record-setting flooding of the Minnesota River in 1993, and again in 1997. But most painful was the March 1998 cell of seven tornadoes that left an estimated $200 million in damage, primarily in Comfrey and St. Peter. Two died, and the path of destruction left scars–some permanent–and suffering for more than a year and a half.

Chronicles of a Century

Part 4

1976 - 1999

Economics reshaped local farming

Many small farmers are pushed out of business; large feedlots emerge

On January 21, 1985, more than 10,000 people converged on the state Capitol in St. Paul in one of the largest protests ever held there. The protesters, many connected with the group Groundswell, demanded a moratorium on farm foreclosures and other programs to help farmers through the Farm Depression of the early and mid '80s.

Agriculture during the last quarter of the century was marked by turmoil, bankruptcy and corporate consolidation.

The ideal of the "family farm" came under constant attack in the late 1970s.

By the early '80s the local farm economy was in ruins. High land prices, low crop prices and double-digit interest rates left many farmers with huge debts they couldn't cover.

As bankruptcy and farm auctions became prevalent, a group called Groundswell was born. A loose-knit group of farmers and activists in western Minnesota began disrupting auctions at farms.

As the movement grew, Bobbi Polzine, a Brewster farm wife, became the fiery spokeswoman for Groundswell.

Groundswell's heyday was Jan. 21, 1985, when more than 10,000 farmers and supporters, including hundreds from the Mankato area, converged on the state Capitol in one of the largest protests ever held there. The protesters asked for a moratorium on farm foreclosures and a grace period on federal loans for troubled farmers.

The protest was partly successful, but the rest of the year was marked by more foreclosures and increased frustration by Groundswell members.

On a bitterly cold morning in December, 10 farmers walked into the Production Credit Association office in Mankato and announced they were taking over. They had no weapons and made no threats.

After seven hours of tense negotiations, the farmers left after being promised a meeting with Attorney General Skip Humphrey and Ag Commissioner Jim Nichols.

That meeting eventually led the 1986 Legislature to enact tougher moratorium laws protecting farmers.

But what became known as the Great Farm Depression forever changed the rural landscape. Most farmers who survived the '80s grew larger and sought new ways to improve efficiency and cushion market fluctuations.

The growth of ethanol and other corn-processing cooperatives was one way farmers sought higher prices for their crops. Ethanol plants, financed by farmer-members and banks, were built in several communities in the late 1980s and early '90s.

The period saw U.S. agriculture become much more dependent on global events and trade. In 1980 the United States imposed a grain embargo against the Soviet Union following its invasion of Afghanistan. The embargo, which depressed farm prices in the United States, was lifted the following year.

Trade agreements with a number of foreign countries were aimed at increasing the free flow of exports and imports, including farm products.

Talks began in late 1986 over GATT, the General Agreement on Tariffs and Trade. Two years later, Canada and the United States signed a free trade accord. And perhaps the most sweeping trade agreement–NAFTA–was ratified in 1993.

Technology continued to alter how farmers do business and dramatically increased production. Satellite technology allows farmers to complete detailed maps of their fields, recording information on fertilizer use, soil condition and crop output.

While it took up to 40 labor hours for a farmer to produce 100 bushels of corn at the start of the century, today's farmer can produce the same amount of corn with one labor hour. Corn yields, about 40 bushels per acre in 1900, now average well over 100 bushels per acre.

Perhaps the most visible and contentious sign of the consolidation in agriculture was the growth of large livestock feedlots. Blue Earth and Nicollet counties became some of the key counties in the state for an explosion in the growth of large hog barns housing thousands of pigs and generating millions of gallons of manure.

Through the 1990s, public debate raged over feedlots. Critics said the manure produced at the feedlots threatened human health and the environment. And they argued that large corporations financing many of the feedlots were squeezing out family farmers. But livestock farmers said they could only stay competitive by becoming larger and more efficient.

The hog industry was shaken in late 1998 and early 1999 by historically low hog prices, leading some producers to quit the business and slowing the construction of new hog feedlots.

A proposed dairy feedlot in Nicollet County became a symbol of the contentious debate over feedlots. The Northern Plains Dairy, which would be the largest in the state, was delayed for years. In 1998, Gustavus Adolphus College filed a lawsuit arguing that the feedlot proposal had not been properly reviewed by the state. In 1999, the project remained under consideration by state and county officials.

First Farmfest drew big names

Presidential candidate Jimmy Carter gave Shari Schroeder, 2, a hug while Senator Hubert Humphrey had a handshake for her brother, Robbie, 7, during their visit to Farmfest in 1976. It was the first year of the event, then held near Lake Crystal.

One of the biggest agriculture shows in the nation began near Lake Crystal in 1976.

The first Farmfest, in September of that year, featured a host of national entertainers and politicians.

Presidential candidate Jimmy Carter, his running-mate Walter Mondale, and Sen. Hubert Humphrey turned out for the event.

While tens of thousands visited the show the first year, it was marred by days of heavy rains and financial problems plagued the promoters.

But the show survived and thrived as it continued near Lake Crystal during the 1980s, drawing 30,000 to 60,000 visitors annually.

In 1990 Farmfest was moved to Austin in an attempt to bolster attendance.

The event was moved again and later held in southwestern Minnesota.

History Glance
1970s

Ottaway buys paper

Jared How sold The Free Press Co. to Ottaway Newspapers Inc. of Campbell Hall, N.Y., a wholly owned subsidiary of Dow Jones & Co. Inc.

Ottaway acquired 11 percent and the remaining 89 percent in 1979.

Through the years The Free Press Co. has also grown and expanded its coverage area. On its 50th anniversary (in 1937) the circulation was about 12,000. By 1962 that figure had grown to 22,000 and by 1970 had reached 24,000. In 1999, the circulation was about 25,000.

Crysteel grows

Crysteel Manufacturing - the Lake Crystal manufacturer of dump truck bodies and hoists for dump trucks - experienced strong sales growth through the 1970s, peaking at $9 million in '79.

Towns cling to schools

As old schools close, communities search for other uses for buildings

In the early part of the century, towns the size of Lafayette were draining students from rural areas, prompting closure of one-room country schools.

By the end of the century, small towns such as Lafayette, Hanska, Pemberton and Garden City were on the other end of that equation.

Many factors were at work: the rural population was declining, many small towns had old buildings needing significant repairs and larger districts had more money to offer a varied program.

Garden City residents–now joined in a school district with Lake Crystal, Amboy and Vernon Center–resisted efforts to build a new school in Lake Crystal in the mid-1990s because it meant closing Wellcome Memorial, a middle school.

Pemberton residents–now joined with Janesville and Waldorf–lost their building because of declining enrollment and the outdated facility. In the early 1990s, Pemberton teachers used multi-age settings–a concept from the old country schools–to boost the number of students in a single classroom.

But Pemberton Elementary closed and the community rallied to convert it to a community center. Hanska and Lafayette residents also tried to find new uses when they lost efforts to keep their small schools open after merging with the New Ulm School District.

In 1999, both communities were working on alternative education plans. Lafayette residents hoped to open a charter school, which is an independent public school run by parents and teachers. Hanska residents hoped to open an arts-based charter school.

History Glance
1970s

Changes at Continental Can

By 1976, Mankato's Continental Can was facing difficulties. Not only had vegetable processors begun to develop their own packaging facilities, but customers preferred a welded can over a soldered one, which the plant specialized in producing.

The company made cutbacks, weeding out obsolete equipment and trimming the workforce by more than 200 employees. At one point, the company had as few as 83 employees.

During the mid to late '70s the plant began to rely more and more upon creating beverage cans, but by the end of 1978, that line was discontinued. New equipment was installed to beef up vegetable canning. The workforce was trimmed again in 1979.

Although rumors circulated about the possible phaseout of the Mankato plant, it escaped that fate.

Schools saw enrollments decline

Consolidation continues but some smaller districts cling to their independence

Technology became paramount in schools during this part of the century. The Knowledge Interactive Distribution System helps small schools increase their program offerings through two-way television.

As schools in Blue Earth and Nicollet counties approached the end of the century, they had to deal with declining enrollment, meet demands for technology and adjust to new educational approaches.

In the 1980s, Minnesota launched several experimental programs to provide students with more choices. Local students could attend any qualifying school district under a new program called open enrollment.

Around the same time, another option emerged that was of particular benefit to local students. The state launched a program in which high school students could take free college classes for credit. With Bethany Lutheran College, Mankato State University and Gustavus Adolphus College within 15 miles of each other, local students had unique opportunities to participate.

A major state initiative to create a standards-based education system challenged local districts. The state's new graduation rule, which required students to demonstrate knowledge in order to graduate, was controversial locally. In Mapleton, a school board member resigned in protest over the state plan, and Nicollet County resident Allen Quist made a second run for the Republican gubernatorial endorsement in 1998 using his opposition to the plan to garner support.

The school choice debate hit Mankato hard in the late 1990s, as supporters of a local charter school sought to open a Mankato school despite opposition from the school board. Charter schools are independent public schools run by teachers and parents.

In the meantime, Mankato Area Public Schools responded to calls for educational options with new programs: it planned to open a Choice School for elementary students seeking nontraditional instruction in 1999, as well as a similar program for middle school students. It also opened a unique model school for chronic truants in the basement of the Law Enforcement Center.

The farm crisis, combined with declining enrollment, took its toll on local schools. Pemberton was one of many towns to lose its school, while residents in Garden City continued to fight a proposal to close Wellcome-Memorial and build a bigger facility in Lake Crystal. Nicollet and St. Clair, however, improved their facilities to reaffirm their commitment to remaining independent districts.

Schools also struggled to come up with money to capitalize on new technology. Computers changed the way students did homework and the Internet opened a new world of information. Teachers had to adapt quickly to find ways to make technology work in the classroom.

St. Peter, Nicollet, St. Clair, Lake Crystal and Cleveland joined a program called the Knowledge Interactive Distribution System, a two-way television system in which the schools could expand program offerings by sharing classes via television. Mankato's schools started a similar interactive program in the late 1990s.

Postsecondary education underwent changes as well. There was a new addition, with Rasmussen Business College opening in 1983. Mankato State University became Minnesota State University, and Mankato Area Vocational-Technical Institute became South Central Technical College with campuses in North Mankato and Faribault. Vo-techs also merged into a system with the state's universities.

Gustavus Adolphus College didn't change its name, but it survived one of the worst natural disasters to strike the region this century. On March 29, 1998, tornadoes swept through St. Peter, causing about $8 million in damage to St. Peter School District's facilities and about $50 million in damage to Gustavus.

The four-year private college rebounded and opened the following fall with 2,450 students, the highest enrollment in its history.

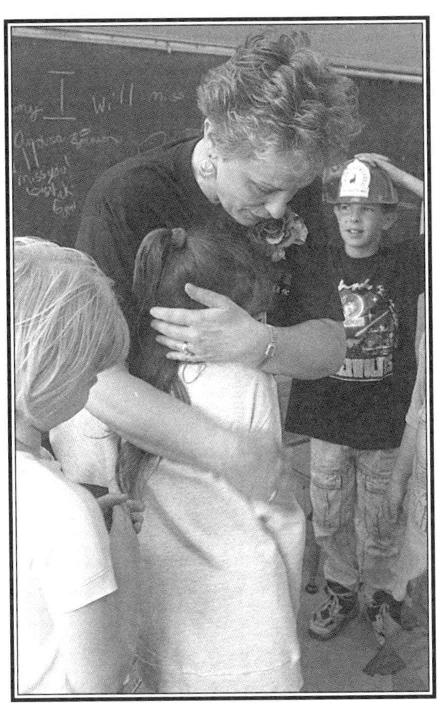

The emotional turmoil of school closings is epitomized in this photo. A Pemberton teacher bids her students farewell on the school's last day in 1995.

History Glance
1980s

Three-wheeling

In 1981, a curious sight could be seen sporting about Mankato's streets: a three-wheeled futuristic car that seated two.

The car, which was licensed as a motorcycle, had a heater, sunroof, carpeting, a single windshield wiper and a radio. It was called a Freeway and its owner, Eugene Lucier of Beauford, bought it after seeing it in a car magazine.

It had a top speed of about 70 mph, and could go 0-60 mph in 13 seconds. But it couldn't go in reverse.

Mankato's oldest retailer closes

Mankato's oldest surviving retailer, Schmidt Saddlery Co., closed in 1986.

The company had been part of Mankato's downtown for 127 years. It evolved from a harness shop into a store carrying a wide array of leather goods, from luggage to belts and purses.

In later years, Schmidt's also sold photographic equipment.

Business bounced back in the '90s

Computer, technical companies offered diverse workforce in Mankato area

Technology, like this diamond-tipped circular saw at Mankato-Kasota Stone, had changed the stone industry in Mankato by 1995. But the owners of the company, the Coughlan brothers, were essentially performing the same service as their great-grandfather – providing a basic building block for an expanding economy.

More than a century of broad, diversified economic development in Mankato continued as the city approached its 150th birthday. Mankato officials long touted the breadth of the local industrial base, leaving the city and its workers with no worrisome dependence on any single firm or industry.

So as the nation went through an energy crisis, the local economy didn't face the devastation seen by oil-dependent places such as Texas. The farm crisis of the 1980s was painful to southern Minnesota, but nonagricultural businesses in the city blunted the impact. And as the economy shifted more toward computer technology and service-related job-creation, growth in Mankato's new computer firms and in its retail and hospitality industry helped the city join the wave.

Which isn't to say that individual companies didn't struggle with the changes.

The national recession of the late 1970s and early 1980s may have hit Kato Engineering as hard as any local firm. The oil industry was a major customer for Kato's generators, which were used in oil drill rigs and refineries. At one point the company laid off 100 workers as plunging oil prices prompted a major reduction in new and existing pumping operations.

Mid-Tex, a manufacturer of relays and transformers, cut its work force of 180 by about 70 people. The company was purchased by Midland Ross in 1980 and in 1986 moved its Mankato production operations to El Paso, Texas, right across the Mexican border. Two hundred local jobs were gone.

Hubbard Milling cut 30 people from its staff of about 240. Midwest Electric Products, which made electrical service outlets, was hurt by the decline in the housing market brought on by extremely high mortgage rates during the recession.

Continental Can, which made tin cans for food products, endured the recession with just one

30-day layoff of about 100 workers, partly because of other cost-cutting measures and partly for a more basic reason.

"People still have to eat," a company official said.

But Ramy Seed Co. filed for bankruptcy in 1982, and the recession nearly delivered a knock-out punch to one of the city's oldest firms, the Dotson Co., born in 1876 as the Lawrence Mayer blacksmith shop. Dotson's customer base was heavily dependent on agriculture and energy–a double whammy in the 1980s. Cheap labor and bad exchange rates made the problem worse as foreign foundries became an attractive option for Dotson's customers.

Sales dropped more than 80 percent, but painful cutbacks–including a decision to stop making the company's trademark Little Giant trip hammer–allowed it to eke through the tough times. By the 1990s, the company had crept back to profitability.

Attempts to bring even more diversity to Mankato's economy also had mixed success. Munsingwear Inc., the nationally known garment manufacturer, and Hormel both looked closely at the city when planning new factories. Both ultimately passed, Munsingware in 1976 and Hormel a couple of years later.

Mankato business owners recognized the coming of the computer age, flooding micro-computer training classes at the Mankato Area Vocational-Technical Institute.

The local construction industry finally saw an upswing in home-buying in 1983 with mortgage rates dropping to under 13 percent. And workers went from seeing unemployment rates of almost 8 percent in 1983 to finding employers nearly begging people to take jobs by the late 1990s.

As companies such as Mid-Tex left Mankato, new startup companies sprang up in their wake. Bob Else, former president of Mid-Tex started E.I. Microcircuits, a maker of computer circuitboards. The company shipped its first product in 1985 and has grown to be one of the area's biggest employers with about 100 employees and $15 million in annual revenues.

Clear With Computers, a maker of software for the automated selling industry, also got its start in the early 1980s and hit a peak employee level of about 350 local employees in 1997. Later that year, the company laid off about 60 employees.

A California technology company announced it planned to acquire CWC in October of 1997, but the deal fell through in January 1998. CWC remains a locally-owned company and employs about 300.

The late 1980s and early 1990s brought a swarm of small-startup companies to Mankato. The city played a role in helping many of them get started with land, buildings and infrastructure.

V-Tek, a maker of electronic-component packaging, and All American Foods, a specialty food ingredient maker, started in the mid-1980s and grew to 40 and 95 employees respectively.

Winland Electronics, a small startup firm in 1976, became a major manufacturer of electronic components with about 100 employees locally.

Although these new firms are subject to the same business cycle ups and downs as older, more established firms, they offered further diversification of the Mankato workbase.

Mankato's Eastwood Industrial Centre, established in the early 1980s, grew in tenants. CWC was joined in the 1990s by Winland Electronics, Atlantis Plastics and Farm Credit Services. Midwest Wireless, a cellular telephone company, also began building a new office complex there in the summer of 1999.

The wireless industry held much hope for the future of the Mankato business scene. A joint effort by industry, Minnesota State University and South Central Technical College helped establish the Global Wireless Education Consortium in Mankato, an industry group including several international wireless companies collaborating to educate wireless workers.

The effort also allowed the schools to collaborate on the Institute of Wireless Education, a separate educational entity operated out of Minnesota State, offering training and classes to wireless workers worldwide.

North Kato hit growth spurt

Retail, residential numbers rise sharply for Nicollet County city

Angie Krech measures type as she inspects an invitation hot off the press at Carlson Craft. The company, which started in the basement of Bill Carlson's West Mankato home, celebrated its 50th anniversary in 1998.

If North Mankato had a theme for the time period of 1976 to 1999, it would have to be growth.

The community saw business and industrial growth, as well as an expanding population that made it one of the fastest growing cities in the region.

"We like to think it's an easy place to do business and an easy place to develop," City Administrator Wendell Sande said. "That makes it an attractive community."

This period saw many new businesses arrive on the hilltop, particularly in the Commerce Industrial Park south of Highway 14.

Printing giant Taylor Corp., beverage bottler Wis-Pack Inc., window fabricator Lindsay Window and Door Co., electronic component manufacturer Thin Film Technology and skin-care producer Sween Coloplast were among the businesses filling out the park.

The Northport Industrial Park north of Highway 14 opened in 1993, with the Northport Center–which now filled–following in 1994.

Then came book publisher Creative Education, printing company Precision Press and another Taylor Corp. company, Great Papers. United Parcel Service soon moved into their new hub facility in the park.

In early 1999, only four acres remained of the original 40-acre park. The city added another 100 acres to Northport in 1998.

Retail development, including banks and now a new grocery store, developed on the hilltop in 1999, with plans for more.

"I think what's happened is that because of the employment base," Sande said, "the service and retail and restaurant business have come along."

The City Council agreed to install sewer, water and streets in growing areas to make land more appealing to developers.

Figures from the Minnesota Department of Economic Security show 12,772 employed in all industries in Nicollet County in 1997. Of those, 5,432 were in manufacturing, an increase of nearly 1,000 jobs since 1993. Total 1997 wages in the county were $289 million.

Backing Sande's take on increasing retail are state numbers showing business services have increased 408 percent in the county from 1993 to 1997, up from 48 units to 244.

Wholesale trade and manufacture of nondurable goods increased 162 percent in the same period from 162 units to 425.

North Mankato's home building continued to boom in the late 1990s, with the Northridge development expanding westward and the Eagle Ridge and Green Acres developments to the north.

The city's population nearly doubled from 1960 to 1997. Residents totaled 5,927 in 1960 and 11,680 in 1997, according to estimates provided by the state demographer.

North Mankato's population was 7,347 in 1970, 9,145 in 1980 and 10,164 in 1990.

"We're looking forward to continued growth," Sande said. "And we're planning the improvements necessary to support that growth."

History Glance
1980s

Celebrity customer

Former Minnesota Viking great Ahmad Rashad doesn't need the big city to get his car fixed. Little old Nicollet did just fine for him in 1980, 1984 and 1992.

Rashad, now a sports commentator for NBC, took his Rolls Royce to John Sieberg, an auto-body repairman from Nicollet, for a paint job. Four years later, Rashad took his yellow Ferrari to Sieberg to get it painted red.

And in 1992, he took it back to Sieberg for another red paint job.

While his car was in the Mankato area, Rashad also stopped at the Option Center to give his car's sound system a boost.

Hickory Tech opens

Hickory Tech Corp. is born in a corporate reorganization, serving as the holding company of Mankato Citizens Telephone Co. and Computoservice.

Mall won shopping contest

Opening of River Hills pulled retailers, customers from city's existing malls

A healthy crowd gathered for the opening of the downtown Mankato Mall in 1978.

The city of Mankato took action to revitalize the downtown during the final quarter of this century.

It launched a bold initiative with the closing of Front Street between Cherry and Hickory streets and enclosing the space to create a downtown mall. When the Mankato Mall opened May 4, 1978, 80 percent of its space was leased.

Paul Meyer, a longtime Mankato businessman, says the mall was an innovative attempt to keep downtown Mankato on the retail map. "It's the only mall of the kind in the U.S. that I know of."

Encouraging signs at Mankato Mall included the expansion of two of its key tenants: Brett's Department Store and JC Penney.

Development in Mankato's hilltop area continued. In May 1979, a Kmart opened. In December 1986, Menards opened.

In the late 1970s, North Mankato looked as though it would enter the fray of new retail development, as well. Fisher/Coughlan & Associates bought 46 acres in North Mankato's hilltop area and proposed to build a 100,000-square foot mall. Its key tenants were to be Fairway Foods, Star Drug, Ben Franklin and Coast-to-Coast.

The city authorized the issuance of $5 million worth of bonds to help finance the project, but the high interest rates of the era made the bond market unattractive. In 1980 interest climbed to 18 percent and rates remained high for the next few years. By 1982, the project was abandoned.

Nevertheless, competition for shoppers would soon intensify with the construction of another shopping center at the junction of Mankato's Madison Avenue and Blue Earth County Road 193.

Some tried to stop the proposed mall. In March 1990, a petition signed by 58 Mankato residents–most with ties to retailers in Madison East or the downtown–was presented to the city opposing the mall.

When it became clear the petition would not slow the project, a lawsuit was filed. Opponents claimed the 77-acre development posed a threat to the environment, but they were unsuccessful in getting a court injunction to stop construction.

The new 600,000-square-foot development, called River Hills Mall, opened Oct. 1, 1991. As of 1999, it was still the biggest shopping center between Sioux Falls, S.D., and Rochester. Retailers at River Hills employed more than 1,000 people.

Among the new tenants the mall brought to town were G.R. Herbergers and Target.

Wal-Mart opened its Madison Avenue store in 1991, as well.

Both Madison East and the Mankato Mall quickly felt the sting of fresh competition.

The Mankato Mall immediately lost one of its anchor businesses - JC Penney - to River Hills.

"The downtown mall had been pretty vibrant until then," Meyer said. "But when Penney's made its decision to move to the top of the hill, it spelled the slow decline of downtown.

"Penney's departure was the crux of that whole thing."

Mankato Mall lost its other anchor–Brett's–in March 1992. Reduced traffic after JC Penney's departure and a snowy winter led to disappointing sales for the 124-year-old Mankato store.

Brett's owner, Brett Taylor Jr., said the store's profits were also hurt by a poor farm economy in the 1980s.

"The downtown mall probably saved our necks for a number of years," Taylor said, but River Hills Mall delivered the crowning blow. "It dramatically sucked business out of the downtown."

Following Brett's departure, tenancy in the mall flagged even more. Subsequently, the owners of Mankato Mall fell behind in paying taxes and rent they owed the city for the land on which the center was built. These missed payments led the city to take over the property itself and hire a management firm, Minnesota Office Investments. Under new management, the Mankato Mall got a new name–Mankato Place.

Meanwhile on the hilltop, Madison East lost Woolworth's in 1993. The store left 45,000 square feet of space in the shopping center.

Scheels All Sports left another hole in Madison East when it relocated to River Hills in 1994.

But the biggest blow for Madison East came with the departure of Sears, its largest single tenant, occupying 87,000 square feet of space. In 1996, Sears moved into River Hills Mall as part of a major expansion there.

Downtown St. Peter businesses felt the effects of Mankato's growing pull as a regional shopping center, too. The city explored the possibility of starting a shopping center of its own in Capital Square. Minnesota lawmakers passed special legislation in 1989, empowering the city to develop land that had previously been set aside for use as a park.

The anchor tenant for the proposed mall–Capitol Square Shopping Center–was to be Pamida. But the project later floundered, and no mall was built.

The opening of the Mankato Civic Center in 1995 helped boost downtown activity. Mankato Place, across the street from the Civic Center, was one of the beneficiaries.

But the Civic Center was no cure-all.

To fill persistent vacancies in Mankato Place, the city converted much of it from retail to office space. In 1998, the city moved its own offices to the mall.

Madison East also moved beyond recruiting exclusively retail tenants to fill space. Besides housing shops, the center became home to offices of all sorts, including a large call- and mail-processing center operated by Young America.

Mankato's east side continued to provide fertile ground for retailers. Menards began building a new store along Thompson Ravine Road in 1999, and several nearby retail/commercial subdivisions were in the works.

River Hills Mall marketing manager Stephanie Harris expected to add another major department store to the mall mix. A new tenant could have up to 128,000 square feet of space.

The project would also involve adding a new corridor to the mall, providing an opportunity for other retailers to gobble up another 40,000 square feet of space.

Shoppers waited as speeches were made at the opening of River Hills Mall in 1991.

Arts scene hit a late high note

Past 25 years had a roller-coaster ride for live entertainment, culture

Live music thrived in the Mankato area throughout the 1970s but hit a down beat in the more conservative '80s.

Arts and entertainment in the Manakto area in these 25 years brought highs and lows that would challenge the most versatile horn player. But the century neared its end on a high note, with an active cultural force and rejuvenated entertainment scene.

Enduring through it all and emerging as one of the area's foremost attractions was the theater at Minnesota State University, a thriving department in the process of expanding with a $2 million black-box theater on campus.

Theater at Mankato State Teacher's College began gaining attention in 1950, when Ted Paul was appointed director. Paul transformed the university's theater output into one that veered from obscure performances to more popular plays.

The success of those plays in drawing audiences led to the construction of the Performing Arts Center in 1967. The 529-seat theater was named the Ted Paul Theatre in 1985.

Paul's desire to have a summer theater in the new center couldn't wait for the building to be completed, so he rented and set up a large tent in front of the new building. The performances were the seeds of what became the Highland Summer Theatre, offering four plays per summer. The Highland Summer Theatre continues today.

In 1980, an independent Department of Theatre Arts was established at MSU, the same time a master of fine arts degree in theater was approved. Paul left in 1980. The department today is chaired by Paul Hustoles.

While the Ted Paul Theatre performed more popular fare, experimental works were adopted by alternative theater groups that were part of the MSU theater scene since 1966.

The Pit Theater was established in 1966, running through 1988. It changed its name to Off Broad Street from 1988 to 1990, and in the 1990-91 season moved to a small location at the Belle Mar Mall, with a new name: Theatre Phoenix.

On Dec. 11, 1995, Mankatoans Lowell and Nadine Andreas gave $1.2 million toward a black box theater at MSU. A fund-raising drive to match the amount was undertaken and groundbreaking took place in the spring of 1998.

Construction was scheduled for the fall of 1999.

A community theater?

In 1982, Gretchen Etzell recruited communitywide to organize a theater group and put on a performance of "Oklahoma."

She was a longtime West High School teacher on leave, and the idea of offering summer classes for children expanded into a community theater idea. She advertised and recruited around town, drawing about 50 members to the summer production in 1982.

The Merely Players was established, and later became a nonprofit organization in 1991, leaving the school district as a funding source and enabling it to receive donations from individual contributors.

The theater continues with drama, comedy and musical productions in the fall, winter and spring.

Live music's ups, downs

In the 1970s, an active art scene at Mankato State University seemed to foster a thriving atmosphere for live music, particularly local acts.

A cluster of downtown bars–the Burgundy House, Hurdy Gurdy, the Square Deal and the Bodega–all offered opportunities for local bands such as City Mouse, the Dust Bowl Blues Band and others.

The 1980s, by contrast, brought with them increasing restrictions–and insurance costs–for establishments that served alcohol, and the live music and downtown entertainment was sparse throughout the decade.

A spark ignited by the Bothy Folk Club in 1990, however, can be traced as the catalyst to a new resurgence of local bands and performers. The Bothy brought together amateur musicians to perform in an open-microphone setting at a small bar above the Oleander called What's Up.

The monthly event drew a large enough crowd that bar manager Mike Pietan decided to establish the small bar as a live music venue. In doing so, he found both a loyal weekend audience as well as a fresh supply of local bands to play. He also tapped into the circuit of traveling bands that charged less.

Others noted his success, and today several bars in the Mankato, St. Peter and the area offer live music every weekend.

While the Bothy Folk Club was taking root in 1990, Mankato resident Ross Gersten pursued the idea of a regional folk festival, organized a group of directors and presented the first Rock Bend Folk Festival at Minnesota Park in St. Peter. The event featured live folk music from area musicians and drew several hundred to the free event.

At the same time, the Nicollet County Historical Society sponsored the first commemorative encampment at the Traverse des Sioux Treaty Site.

Both events took place annually on fall weekends through 1998, after which the encampment was canceled. The state Historical Society, which owned the property, planned a renovation of the area. The encampment attracted an average of 9,000 visitors during each of its eight annual weekends and some state Historical Society members were concerned about maintaining the natural integrity of the area. Trail construction, area upgrade and planting were scheduled to be completed by June 30, 2001.

The folk festival continued each fall, growing in the caliber of acts offered. Past performers included Lucy Kaplansky, John Hartford and Peter Ostroushko.

The heavy hitters

The opening of the Mankato Civic Center in 1995 was the most significant local entertainment event of the 1990s.

The Civic Center's management brought stadium-level concerts to the area, frequently tapping into tours that would otherwise hit the Twin Cities and leave the area. The Civic Center often had shows exclusive of the metro area.

Among its hit performers: Bob Dylan; Crosby, Stills and Nash; Aerosmith; Kiss; Alan Jackson; and Vince Gill.

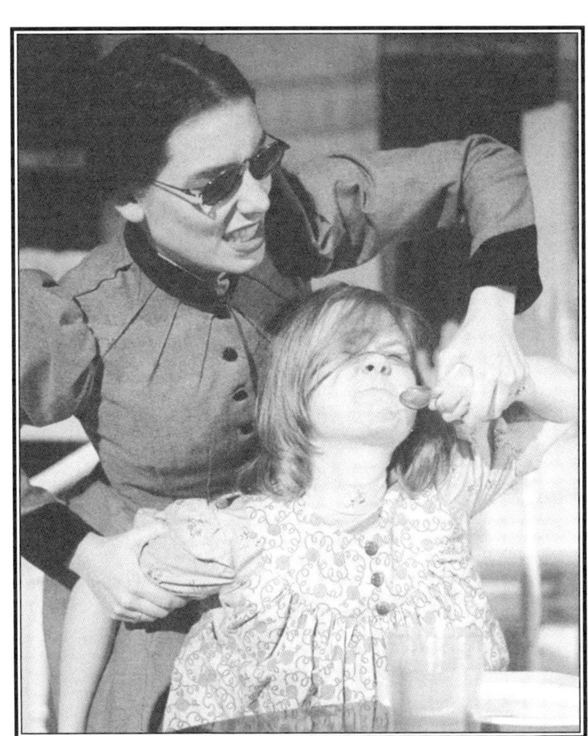

Mankato State University's theater department remained a solid artistic venue in the community during this 25 years. In the late 1960s, its director moved the department from obscure to more popular works such as 'The Miracle Worker.'

Roads were a driving force

Highway 169 gets a number of makeovers, as does Highway 14

It was 1986 when the Veterans Memorial Bridge underwent construction. The bridge, rebuilt twice since the turn of the century, provided a vital link between Mankato and North Mankato.

Many people moved from gas guzzlers to three-cylinder engines, governments refined the art of infrastructure, and more people chose biking or walking to work in the last quarter of the 20th century.

Roadways in the Mankato region got facelifts between 1976 and 1999, with several major road projects still under construction in 1999.

One of the area's main arteries, Highway 169, saw several upgrades, including a major one in the early 1990s that eased flow through the Mankato area, and another major one between 1996 and 1998 that refurbished the roadway between Mankato and St. Peter.

Another project, conceived in the late 1980s, used $14 million to build a 9.4-mile highway running east to west, south of Mankato.

The South Route was designed to quell traffic congestion in the core Mankato-North Mankato area, and make bypassing the region quicker and easier for motorists traveling around Mankato.

Most of those motorists, incidentally, exchanged the V-8 engines of the 1960s for fuel-efficient compact cars or, later, for luxury minivans and sport utility vehicles.

Highway 14, another major highway for the region, saw major change in this period. Highways 14 and 169 were the only two area highways, after a 1996 law change, allowing motorists to legally travel 65 mph (on four-lane sections only).

Highway 14, however, has carried the dubious distinction of being one of the area's most deadly highways. Its dangerous reputation prompted the Legislature to fund upgrading it from two to four lanes. About a third of the project, which aims to extend the four-lane upgrade from Mankato to Waseca, was complete by 1999.

The Mankato Airport was a major political issue, especially deciding who should pay for renovation. After a lengthy debate about funding improvements among several local governments, the Mankato City Council decided to use sales tax revenue to upgrade the facility.

Perhaps because of a heightened level of environmental awareness, more people reverted to transportation modes reminiscent of earlier times: walking and biking.

New bike shops opened, catering to a surge in demand for two-wheeled transportation.

Responding to that trend, governments became more willing to spend money on trail systems. The Red Jacket Trail, which runs south of Mankato, and the Sakatah Trail, which starts north of town and stretches 40 miles to Faribault, were attracting local residents and tourists.

Buses remained a hot topic in the late 1970s, although the focus shifted from whether or not to have buses, to how to get people to ride them. Ridership slumped and in 1978, the city sought marketing help to get more people riding buses.

By the 1990s, ridership had stabilized and buses were catering to non-motorized travelers. Bike racks now adorned the grills of some municipal buses.

Not to be outdone, in 1978 the first passenger jets came to Mankato offering flights to Chicago.

The service's debut came April 30 when 22 Mankato residents boarded for the route's maiden flight. After a brief stop in Rochester, the jet flew to Chicago in about an hour and a half.

By 1999, however, Mankato had no commercial air carrier.

Cities dueled for Kato Engineering

After being a Mankato fixture for 55 years, Kato Engineering took its business to North Mankato in 1981.

But before its new $7.5 million plant was built, officials from Mankato and North Mankato went head-to-head to compete for the business.

In 1980, the company announced it was considering sites in both cities for its new plant. That prompted the city of Mankato to approve a $10 million industrial revenue bond sale in anticipation of construction on Third Avenue.

Kato Engineering also was considering a site in the southern part of the country as well. Ultimately, the plant ended up locating off Highway 14 and Lookout Drive in North Mankato, much to the chagrin of Mankato officials.

The new plant came not long after Kato Engineering was purchased by Reliance Electric, an Ohio-based manufacturer of electro-mechanical motors, controls and power transmission devices.

In 1979, Reliance was purchased by Exxon Corp., a multi-national petroleum company.

Interestingly enough, 75 percent of the company's sales in 1981 were tied to oil drilling and refining operations.

The changing face of churches

Evolvement of joint churches and charismatic movement marked change

Ecumenism may be the watchword for church evolvement in the latter part of the century.

In 1976, three Mankato congregations–Centenary Methodist, First Baptist and First Congregational–joined to build the Multi-Church Center at Second and Cherry streets.

Under the arrangement, each congregation could hold services in either of two sanctuaries, and all shared operating and maintenance costs. This unique operation attracted national attention.

Ecumenism of another sort proliferated in the mid-1970s when the charismatic renewal movement gained strength among area Christians.

The movement, whereby practitioners sometimes speak in tongues or witness their faith through other highly emotional actions, was welcomed by some mainstream Christians for the vitality and joy it seemed to evince and eyed warily by others, who saw it as unthinking fundamentalism.

By 1989 there were more than 40 churches in Mankato/North Mankato, and ecumenical and joint services had become common.

Not so common was the Catholic Church of St. Peter's interim pastor several years earlier. The Rev. David Cawkwell of England, who described himself as an "ecclesiastical dropout," was perhaps emblematic of the divergent routes taken to ordination in the late part of the century in American churches.

Cawkwell said he had flitted from Sunday School to Sunday School as a child, exposing himself to various beliefs before turning Catholic at age 18.

Prior to the priesthood, he had worked in government and done volunteer work with the deaf. He said a parish priest is peripheral to his congregation.

"Priests come and go, but most people in a parish stay. So what goes on, they must have a very large say in."

Another non-traditional church development occurred in 1990, when Trinity Church of Mankato moved into a huge vacated industrial warehouse along Highway 169.

The metal-sided building was decidedly mundane, but Pastor Cleon Laughlin was able to look beyond it.

"The day of the crystal cathedral is over," he said. "Most people don't want to put their money into stained glass windows and a half-million dollar pipe organ."

In 1993, the Church of St. Peter experienced instant growth when it merged with St. Mary's

Catholic of St. Peter. The latter's building was razed to make room for a supermarket.

In 1998, the Catholic Church of St. Peter had to be razed following extensive tornado damage in March. A new church was be built on the northwest edge of town.

Social consciousness and the church also comingled in this period, and at times the outcomes were sobering.

In 1985, St. John's Catholic in Mankato, which routinely left its doors open to harbor the homeless, was victimized by the theft of $3,000 worth of silver and gold chalices.

An anonymous citizen tipped police to the thief, a man recently released from prison. The items were recovered and the man was arrested.

In 1993, Winona Catholic Diocese Bishop John Vlazny, addressing the hurt caused by sexual misconduct of clergy, personally conducted "healing" services in Mankato and other diocesan cities.

The 1990s also produced an abundance of small "niche" churches catering to people who, for various reasons, didn't find themselves served by mainstream parishes.

The Christian Life Center in Mankato, for example, was founded to meet the needs of young people who shun traditional church settings. The church incorporates rock music into its worship services and operates an adjoining cafe catering to high school and college-age patrons.

St. Peter State Hospital became Treatment Center

Trends toward more community-based treatment of the mentally ill brought a continuing decline in the number of people in state facilities such as the St. Peter State Hospital.

But with the Rochester State Hospital closing in 1981, the St. Peter facility became responsible for any care needed by another 400,000 people living in 10 southeastern Minnesota counties. The wider service area doubled admissions to the St. Peter State Hospital and resulted in a new name in 1985: St. Peter Regional Treatment Center.

An expansion at the Moose Lake Regional Treatment Center later drew away many of the St. Peter facility's most dangerous patients, called psychopathic personalities.

The damage was devastating

Two people died, more than 3,000 structures hit or destroyed by tornadoes

Harmon Glass workers begin the long task April 1, 1998, of replacing the blown out windows of North, Link and Sorensen Halls at Gustavus Adolphus College.

It was difficult, if not impossible, to grasp the enormity of the disaster that hit south-central Minnesota on Sunday, March 29, 1998.

Two people died, dozens were injured and more than 3,000 homes, businesses and farm structures were damaged, hundreds destroyed.

The damage estimate was close to $200 million, with some $75 million of that in farm damage.

But no statistics, no amount of media coverage could portray the harshness and extent of damage done by the spectacular tornadoes that tore across eight counties.

Shortly after 4 p.m. the storm demolished the small town of Comfrey and hundreds of farms. Then rural Hanska. Then the Cambria and Judson areas.

The storm pulled out of the river valley, bypassing Mankato as it headed for St. Peter shortly after 5 p.m.

When the tornadoes hit the top of the bluff overlooking St. Peter, they still packed 200 mph force. They ripped through Gustavus Adolphus College, descended into the heart of the city and moved on in a matter of minutes.

The storm headed east, destroying a mobile home park and damaging other buildings in Le Center.

Stunned and relieved

Afterward, rural residents found every building, animal and piece of equipment had blown away at some farm sites; large groves were reduced to twisted stumps.

Comfrey residents saw virtually every business and home destroyed beyond repair.

In St. Peter, stunned residents found carnage in every direction. All electrical power was out. Trees were toppled onto homes, streets and vehicles. Debris and glass were strewn everywhere.

But, in spite of its fury, the storm had injured and killed far fewer people than the damage would indicate.

Six-year-old Dustin Schneider was killed when his family's van was swept from a road near St.

Peter, and Louis Mosenden, 85, died from injuries when the storm hit his rural Hanska farm home.

Pulling together

Shock quickly gave way to cleaning up and supporting victims.

By Monday, local, state and federal agencies had set up temporary command posts and emergency assistance stations

Three days after the storms, President Clinton declared four counties as disaster areas, clearing the way for federal disaster aid. The Minnesota Legislature began putting together a $28 million aid package of its own.

Residents, government crews and friends and relatives of victims had the worst of the debris and trees off the roads by Monday evening. As the scope of the damage was spread by the state and national media, volunteers and charitable organizations inundated the communities with offers of assistance.

By late week, some 85 percent of the debris had been cleared out of St. Peter. Cleanup in the rural areas was slower, as muddy conditions prevented clearing debris from tens of thousands of acres of farm fields.

The weekend after the storm was the pinnacle of the volunteer effort. Nearly 2,000 alumni and students descended on Gustavus Adolphus College to clean the grounds; buses carrying some 3,000 more volunteers from across the state came to help.

Family of tornadoes

The National Weather Service determined a "super cell thunder storm" spawned a "family" of seven tornadoes, with widths of one to five miles.

Unlike most Minnesota tornadoes, which appear in May and June, touch down for only a short distance and disappear, super-cell storms create new tornadoes after the previous ones die down.

Personal stories

The thousands of personal stories of survival, heroics and fear will never by fully detailed. But in the week following the tornadoes, victims shared some of their stories with friends and the media:

A rural Hanska farmer, Dean Schneider, was in the farm yard with his two sons when a tornado hit. Hunkered down behind a short concrete-block wall, Schneider began seeing barn doors and other debris blow past. Then he looked up to see a sight that many believed was only a figment of Hollywood's imagination in the movie "Twister"–one of Schneider's dairy cows sailed over his head and out into a field.

In St. Peter, Mike Skrove was actually watching the movie "Twister" with his sons Dustin and Jordan. His wife, Sheila, was resting upstairs when she heard the sirens and came down to ask why they weren't taking shelter.

"We just thought it was the movie," Mike Skrove said. The family headed to the basement just before their house was lifted up and tossed into the next block.

Residents along North Fourth Street in St. Peter were shocked as they looked out the side of their rooms. The storm took off the side of the house.

A neighbor later found Skrove's VCR a block away, pried out the "Twister" videotape with a screwdriver and gave it to Skrove as a souvenir.

Doug Steffl was just getting his Comfrey home back in shape after a fire three months before. On Sunday night he watched a black cloud turn to white columns and headed for the basement. "When it hit, water just started shooting out of cracks in the basement floor and the whole house started bouncing."

A few families, trapped outside, reported watching helplessly as a child or spouse was pulled into the air and disappeared. Amazingly, all were dropped a short distance away without sustaining life-threatening injuries.

Looking to the future

Most of Comfrey's 450 residents decided to rebuild their homes and businesses. In St. Peter, concern focused on damage to the large number of historically significant buildings–many dating to the 1850s.

Even with insurance and disaster aid, many farmers found it impossible to start over. But thanks to dry weather and volunteers, debris was cleaned from thousands of acres of fields before spring planting.

Le Center resident Josefina Arroyo, whose family lost their home, summed up the feeling of many victims who lost only buildings and belongings.

Looking at her two children and husband, Benito, Josefina said: "It would have been worse if something had happened to them, but I have everybody. And that's the main thing."

Sarah Jeliff, a Gustavus Adolphus College student, pauses from salvaging personal belongings in her St. Peter apartment that was destroyed by a tornado that passed through the community March 29, 1998.

St. Peter school succumbed to spring tornadoes

For years, it seemed nothing could overcome public support to save the aging St. Peter Central School.

But in 1998, spring tornadoes destroyed what budget-crunching, space studies and administrative recommendations couldn't.

St. Peter's Central Community Center was another victim of the storm.

Built in 1907, the Central Annex served students in grades one through 12. A separate high school section was added in 1907, and enrollment prompted another addition in 1926.

School officials began to point out its age in the 1970s. (By then, it was an elementary school. A new junior and senior high had been built in 1956.) Central wasn't handicapped accessible, and it wasn't energy efficient. Repairs would be costly.

But parents and graduates convinced the school board to keep it open.

Instead of closing the building, handicapped students were moved from the Annex to the Central building.

The solution was temporary. Faced with expensive repair bills and a report that the district could save $100,000 a year in operating expenses, the board closed the Annex in 1977 and Central Elementary in the 1980-81 school year.

The decision was made despite a petition with more than 800 signatures urging the board to keep it a school.

Instead of demolishing it, the facility became the Central Community Center. It housed organizations ranging from city offices to the senior center to a day care. Community members continued to use its gym.

The March 29, 1998, disaster left the building in ruins.